Copyright © 2024 Rebecca J. Barkhouse
Published by Silvden Communications, through The Language Navigator.

All rights reserved. This book or parts thereof may not be reproduced in any form, stored in any retrieval system, or transmitted in any form by any means, electronic, mechanical, photocopy, recording, or otherwise, without prior written permission of the publisher, except as provided by United States of America copyright law. For information regarding permission requests, write to rbarkhouse@languagenavigator.com, Attention: Permissions Coordinator.

ISBN	eBook	978-1-0689372-2-4
	Paperback	978-1-0689372-0-0
	Hardcover	978-1-0689372-1-7

First Edition
Book Production and Publishing by Brands Through Books
brandsthroughbooks.com

By reading this document, the reader agrees that under no circumstances is the author or the publisher responsible for any losses, direct or indirect, which are incurred as a result of the use of information contained within this document, including, but not limited to, errors, omissions, or inaccuracies.

LEGAL NOTICE:
This book is copyright protected. Please note the information contained within this document is for educational and personal use only. You cannot amend, distribute, sell, use, quote, or paraphrase any part, or the content within this book, without the consent of the author or publisher.

https://languagenavigator.com

Unlocking Exceptional *You*

How to **Cultivate the Mindset, Habits, and Skills to Achieve Your Professional Dreams**

REBECCA J. BARKHOUSE

SILVDEN COMMUNICATIONS
Nova Scotia, Canada

Praise for *Unlocking Exceptional You*

"Rebecca taught many groups of students who were preparing to study flight skills in English-speaking countries, such as Canada, the US, and Australia. She helped prepare them culturally as well as technically while consistently working with each student's English. We've appreciated her motivation and dedication to her students' success."

Jack Du, CAMIC, China, 2012 to 2016

"Rebecca Barkhouse is one of the best teachers in Flying College Beihang University, and one of the most popular teachers among all the students, but first and foremost, she is a considerate, helpful, and warmhearted teacher. She gained the honor 'Annual Excellent Teacher of Beihang University' of year 2015 based on the fact that her class is so attractive [to] her students. Also in year 2016, she was the only foreign teacher on the name list of the program of 'I love My Teacher' in Beihang University. She prepared for lessons carefully and imparted them with passion so that student attendance was incredibly high. She is a person of discipline and has a strong abidance [to] punctuality, making her an extremely good example of a wonderful pilot to all the students in Flying College."

Wang Dan, Foreign Assistant of Flying College, Beihang University, China, 2007 to 2016

"Rebecca was a huge inspiration to us in China. All flight instructors can teach theory but not all instructors can inspire."

Xu Chen, Undergraduate student, Beihang University, China, 2008 to 2009

"Rebecca helped break down the information into understandable pieces so that I could build them back into theory that made sense to me. She didn't just give me the information but let me figure it out with her guidance so that I comprehended it and didn't just memorize it."

Ricky Richard, CPL student, Canada, 2023

"Rebecca is exceptional at simplifying complex topics and making them easily understandable. One of her standout strengths is her ability to take intricate, challenging concepts and present them in a way that just clicks, using teaching methods that work for me (i.e., visual aids and diagrams). Her patience and practical explanations were incredibly beneficial to me during my preparation for my CPL exam."

Molly Christensen, CPL student, Canada, 2023

To my family, Bruce Barkhouse, Ruthann Barkhouse, and Ramona and Jason Aitchison, for their unwavering support, and in memory of my mother, Gwen Barkhouse, who would have encouraged me to never give up!

CONTENTS

Chapter 1. **Dreaming Big and Finding Direction**   3

Chapter 2. **A Strong Foundation: The Why and Defining Success**   17

Chapter 3. **ACE the RISK™ Wheel: Framework for Success**   27

Chapter 4. **ACE the RISK™ Wheel, Applied to Aviation**   35

Chapter 5. **R—Relationships: How You Fit in Your World**   43

Chapter 6. **I—Industry: The World You Are Entering**   53

Chapter 7. **S—Situations: Day-to-Day Tasks and Lessons**   75

Chapter 8. **K—Keynotes: Making the Job Your Own**   83

Chapter 9. **E—Evaluate: Coming Full Circle**   91

Chapter 10. **Completing the Circle**   111

Education is not the learning of facts but the training of the mind to think!

—*Albert Einstein*

Dear Reader,

My name is Rebecca Barkhouse. I'm a pilot, Class 1 flight instructor, and an individual who loves life and always seeks adventure. I want to share with you a journey—my journey of taking my childhood dream and making it a reality. I'll share all the lessons learned along the way and introduce a basic framework to help you achieve your dreams of becoming a professional, thrive in your chosen career, and be successful in any learning journey you are on or any situation you encounter in your life where you can be an exceptional human being!

I was born in the small town of Bridgewater in Nova Scotia, a province on the east coast of Canada that is very picturesque. I grew up in an idyllic setting—or so it seems now, looking back on it. I had wise and patient parents, and my sisters and I had a wealth of outdoor activities we could do, along with any hobbies that took our fancy. My journey to becoming a pilot started in this small town, on my parents' property, with my older sister beside me...

As a little girl, I was always on the move, and usually at high speeds. There were many times my bicycle and I had disagreements—I typically came out worse than the bicycle! I had big brown eyes, big brown ringlets, and a really big heart for dreaming; my mom called me the daydreamer, and she wasn't wrong. I was always thinking about other things besides what I should have been doing at the moment. In this mental environment, my biggest dream was born, one that would mold my future. It's been several years since I was that little girl with a big dream, and I have learned that, although all training programs and instructors aren't created equal, if you have the desire, ambition, and guidance, you will succeed. This book will give you the system, tools, and direction to achieve success. It introduces a framework and practical examples for you to use as you start on your learning, dream-achieving, and practical skill development journey. We can't control the external environment or how we get our instruction, but we can prepare and control ourselves! I use my history of studying, teaching, and making mistakes as the foundation to pass on knowledge, personal preparation habits, learning methods, and successful mindset techniques through a framework developed from observed patterns and my experience as both a student and instructor.

The premise of this book is based on the assumptions I live life by:

1. Success requires work, motivation, and perseverance.
2. Obstacles to overcome will arise.
3. Patience is required, even with yourself.
4. Find your strengths but accept no one is strong in everything.
5. Learning is a journey, not a destination.

So, with these assumptions, let's start on the path of getting ready to learn and cultivate the mindset, habits, and skills to become the professional you want to become. Together, we will go over how to build a solid foundation, identify and establish tools to maintain your path, and be aware of the big picture. My path has been messy, indirect, and frustrating but, in reflection, necessary for my progress thus far, and my wish is to use my experience to help your journey be a little smoother!

Sincerely yours,
Rebecca

CHAPTER 1

DREAMING BIG AND FINDING DIRECTION

A Seed Is Planted

It was a beautiful summer day in Nova Scotia; the sun was beaming down, and a light breeze was blowing. My older sister and I were in our parents' vegetable garden, helping with the weeding, when an airplane flew over us. Always looking for a reason to take a break from weeding, we heard the low rumble above us and looked up to see the small airplane fly over. My dad had a friend who was a pilot, so as children with linear logic, this was obviously dad's friend. We ran to the end of the garden so we could wave furiously and yell, "Hello!" At that moment, age seven or eight, I knew I wanted to be a pilot when I grew up—and so the seed was planted!

Some of us know what we want to do at a young age, but for others, it takes some time to figure it out. I have an important point to bring up here: reflect on your childhood and think about what you really liked to do, what you were good at, and what made you happy while doing it. These are all strong indicators of what career you would thrive in. A child has the advantage of less distraction and a purity in their thoughts; this is why I believe the seed is planted at a young age but isn't recognized until later.

Throughout the next decade of my life, I learned to adapt to change, adjusting to life in junior high and high school while also keeping my grades up and thinking about my future, as we all do during that period of our life. One thing that helped me when I got discouraged was the idea that I would be able to live my dream someday. The struggle with having a dream is that reality has a way of bringing you back to earth and making the dream seem further and further away. I knew very few pilots, and it wasn't a career that many people had or knew about, but there was a tenacious hold on that seed planted in my heart as a child, and it was growing.

Your Support People

I finally reached grade twelve, and my future loomed ahead of me with hope and a bit of dread. I really had no idea what I wanted to do with my life. I knew I wanted to be a pilot, but that option seemed so far away I wanted to look at other possibilities for career as well. To gain some hope and direction, I went to the school guidance counselor. I walked into his office, where the blinds were drawn and there was a sense of calm and quiet, the perfect atmosphere to talk about the heavy decisions of the future. I sat down, looked at Mr. Grey, and said, "I have no idea what I want to do with my life, but I *do* know what I don't want to do. I don't want to work in a place where I have to sit in the same four walls every single day!"

He responded with, "Well that gives us a place to start!" He proceeded to set me up with the True Colors Test to determine my personality and therefore a list of careers that would be a good fit for my personality. On that list were pilot and teacher, among other things, but those two stuck out for me. It is so important to have people in your life who support you and help you sort through all the noise to find your passion. It could be friends, family, teachers, or guidance counselors. Sometimes it's even a random interaction with a stranger or a song or a video you have watched. Use these situations to build a strong foundation so you have that support when you need it.

I was now armed with the knowledge that being a pilot was a good fit for my personality. I needed to find out more information on what was required to become a pilot, where the schools were, and when it was possible to start. Luckily enough, a few months later, we had a career day at school and representatives from different universities and colleges within Canada came with presentations on what their institutions offered. Moncton Flight College gave a presentation, and I went to listen and gather information. Three of us attended and found out the requirements for starting school to become a pilot. Math and physics were required, as well as a high school certificate, but the biggest obstacle was that the schooling cost quite a bit of money. Doing research or finding information on your field of interest assists in starting to build a plan for your future. It is important to learn the process and what you are getting involved in. A big point to remember here is that just because something is hard or will take a long time doesn't mean it isn't worth it; it will just take time, and in that time, you will develop your skills and expertise.

I went home with my information package and told my parents what I had learned and what I thought the biggest obstacle was, which was finances. We talked about it together and thought on it for a few days. We collectively decided it would be too expensive to do right out of high school. My older sister was doing a secondary education course, and flight school in 2000 required $56,700 for tuition for two years, plus living expenses and incidentals. I was disappointed but also understood. At the time, getting adequate government student loans for flight school was difficult because universities and colleges were the most recognized benchmark for tuition amounts for loans per year. One year of flight school was equivalent to at least two years of university tuition. The student loans I eventually did get did not meet the tuition requirement, so a bank loan was also required. Just out of high school, I couldn't raise that amount of money personally, so the dream went on the shelf for a while.

Adjusting the Plan

As a plan B, I chose to get other schooling and went to the community college in my town to study hospitality services. It was a two-year course that taught me all the ins and outs of the hospitality industry. With that diploma, I worked at a hotel in Nova Scotia for a year and then ended up in Western Canada, at Lake Louise, Alberta. The hotel I worked at was nestled in the Rocky Mountains; it was absolutely gorgeous, and the mountains were phenomenal. Living in those mountains made me think, *If God can make those mountains, anything is possible for me.* It was basically a moment of decision: Would I take the easy road and work at hotels the rest of my life, or would I take the unfamiliar, uncomfortable road that would lead me to my dream of becoming a pilot, which I'd had since I was a child? After several days of heavy thinking, I decided to move forward and contact the school to start the process. I felt a sense of contentedness: I was actually going through with this dream!

I applied to Moncton Flight College and got accepted on the condition that I'd take a high school physics course online. Working in the mountains, two hours from the biggest city, I started online physics. This required me to rent a computer and use it in my dorm room at Lake Louise. I ended up finishing the course at home after I moved back to Nova Scotia. I moved back earlier than I planned due to a family illness, as my mother was diagnosed with cancer. I wanted to help take care of the family and my mom while she was sick. This decision delayed my training, but I wouldn't have had it any other way, because my priorities had changed.

This delay was hard to come to terms with on many levels; it was hard to delay pursuing the dream, bringing up the question of whether I should keep the faith for the dream even though it seemed further away. It was also emotionally taxing because my mother was terminally ill. There were many memories that happened in the six months I was home. It was desperately hard, but there were bonds forged that are irreplaceable. She passed away that July, and the process of grief started, a necessary process to go through, and one which doesn't obey the bounds we set for it.

Testing My Faith in the Dream

The one thing you learn when you take the path of catching dreams is that there will be obstacles and delays. During these times, it is confusing, there is doubt, and it's hard to deal with. However, I personally use these setbacks as an opportunity to check in with myself and reflect on whether I am on the right path. I take some time to go over what brought me to this point in my life. What encouragement started me on this path? Is that encouragement still valid? For example, I still had my dream from being a little girl who wanted to fly. Yes, still valid! I still had that realization from Lake Louise that anything was possible. Also, still valid! So, was this enough to make me keep going? Yes, it was! These two things, as well as other subtle nudges, established I was on the right path, just not right now. Obstacles will disappoint and discourage you. Take the time to feel that feeling but also know that you now have the time and space to reassess the situation. It's time to make a decision: either recommit to continue pursuing the dream or stop altogether. The decision has to be right for your life and the stage you are at. If you have confirmation that you are on the right path, let it strengthen your resolve to keep going.

Returning to my personal story, we'll fast forward a year. I had returned to Lake Louise to work for five months to make some money before I started school. After my five months of working, I arrived in Moncton, New Brunswick, to start flight school, four days late due to my work contract with Chateau Lake Louise. But I was finally there and ready to start the actual learning journey.

The flight college I chose to attend offered several programs, which I will cover in depth in chapter six. I chose to do the two-year diploma program the college offered. The training had its ups and downs, and there were more obstacles and points when decisions turned into opportunities for confirmation again. My first year, at Christmastime, I was delayed again due to a family friend having a major motor vehicle accident. I took leave to go and be a support person for the family. I missed my chance to do my private pilot license written exam. I returned to school after the holidays and caught up by doing the written exam. Then, on a school break in March, I broke my leg skiing. So there I was, delayed again. This delay was three months long, as I had a cast for six weeks and then a brace for another six weeks. Being this far behind gave me the resolve to put my head down and make up for the very large gap I had to overcome on the timeline of training. This is another example of using delays and obstacles to decide to keep pursuing my dream. I had a taste of what could be my career, and I couldn't let a broken leg and a month and a half of delay derail my progress.

An interesting observation I made during my time chasing dreams was that I had a similar pattern of problems. I had financial problems, harbored self-doubt in my ability, and was hesitant about long-term commitment to success when learning new material. These problems kept coming up over and over. Using the pressure of being behind, I completed my flight time in six weeks and was caught up with my class and ready to start the second year in record time. The major difference was my mindset: I committed and resolved to make it work.

Regardless of what industry you choose, are in, or are transitioning to, there will be obstacles and times of discouragement. There will be times when you will have to reflect on your foundation of decisions and encourage yourself. Have you dealt with this in your life before? I would suspect that you have already dealt with these situations in your life and have experienced both sides of dealing with an obstacle and the negative and positive impacts. Always remember that making a less-than-ideal decision will lead to an opportunity to make another decision.

The second year was a bit smoother, but money was running short, which brought up the obstacle of finances to overcome again. Family members stepped in and helped me fill the financial gap. But in the end, I graduated with honors with all my licenses. Whew, what a relief! It was so wonderful to see the realization of a dream. Walking across the stage to receive my diploma was so satisfying.

A week after graduation, I moved to Manitoba to work at a fishing lodge for four months. In return, I received ten hours of training for my float rating, an endorsement on my pilot license that allows me to land and take off on water, and twenty-five hours of float flying experience. It was a wonderful, busy summer. I built great friendships, got my float rating, and did a lot of fishing.

Finding the First Stepping Stone

Once a person gets their pilot's licenses, the hunt is on for the first job to build up flight hours and become employable to larger companies. As with every industry, there is a hierarchy that has to be navigated to reach the top. In the aviation industry, flight hours are the golden prize and what each new pilot strives for; therefore, most find a job that will get them flight hours in a short time so they can move to a bigger company with bigger aircraft, then from first officer to captain. There is a lot of career movement in this industry. In Canada, the two most common ways to get flight hours are becoming a flight instructor, which requires more training, and working at a smaller company, likely in the northern parts of Canada, as a ground handler, fueler, etc. Eventually, the pilot gets a first officer position. Of these two options, I chose flight instructor and returned to Moncton Flight College to take my instructor rating and learn to teach. I enjoyed doing the course, and it consolidated a lot of lessons I had learned in other jobs where I trained colleagues. It was an opportunity to solidify all previous lessons into what would become my teaching pattern. After doing the course, there were no jobs for instructing, so I worked as a dispatcher at the college for almost a year.

I was thrilled when Moncton Flight College signed a contract with Beihang University in Beijing, China, to train student pilots in Moncton so they could return and work for the major airlines in China. With this influx of students, my first flight students were Chinese student pilots who were brave enough to take up the challenging and daunting task of learning to fly in a foreign country and in their nonnative language.

It was amazing to learn about the differences between Canadian and Chinese cultures and how this affected the learning/teaching relationship. The expectations of the students and instructors were different, and this caused some frustrations on both sides. But it gave the instructors and students an opportunity to learn how to adapt and grow in the process. An example of this difference when teaching is that the students didn't want to ask questions because it was viewed as disrespectful to the teacher, insinuating the teacher wasn't doing a proper job. But when I teach, I want students to ask questions because I may have missed a small detail that will give the proper context and therefore help with comprehension. If no one asks questions, I move on and assume the class understands the information. This can lead to problems. For example, if the student needs to execute a procedure for a maneuver according to the procedure sequence, based on theory taught in the classroom, and it is not understood correctly, then it is done incorrectly. This leads to frustration on both sides because the instructor thought the student understood the theory correctly and the student was unsure how they were incorrect. The student feels lost, and the instructor doesn't understand why the student isn't preforming because they thought the student understood. As you can see, this doesn't support a healthy learning/teaching environment. The key point is not to stop at the frustration stage and instead work through it and find ways to solve this problem. A couple of solutions that resulted from this situation were to make it very clear to the students that it was okay to ask questions as well as make them feel comfortable asking the questions, even if it was after class. Also, as the instructor, I learned to ask more questions after a concept was taught. By doing this, I could pick up on the general understanding of the class and know if I had to reteach it or if I could move on. This became a very useful tool in all my teaching, whether in a large class or one-on-one teaching.

Another example of the cultural differences is how we say, "I understand." If someone was teaching me a concept and then asked me if I had questions, I would say, "No, I understand." When I would teach a new concept to my Chinese students, at the end, sometimes they would say, "I know." At first, I interpreted this to mean they already knew the concept, but what they actually meant was, "*Now* I understand." That also took me some time to get used to, and I would ask them questions to ensure they understood the material correctly. In the end, it takes both the students and instructors to have a successful learning /teaching experience! The following is an aviation-specific example of this miscommunication and misalignment of expectations.

One day, as I was walking out of the flight operations building, I looked up and saw two aircraft quite close to each other in the sky. I thought to myself, *That was a little close. I'll have to check into that.* I finished the task I was on my way to do and then went back to the dispatch desk to find out who was flying. To my surprise, it was my student, and he had followed the procedure I had taught him correctly. The student ahead of him in the traffic circuit had also followed the procedure he was taught perfectly. The procedures were the same, but the timing on when to do the steps was vague; one student was taught to turn left at one thousand feet above the airfield, and the other student was taught to turn left at six hundred feet above the airfield. This made the aircraft too close when they had to make the next left turn. Neither student was incorrect, they were following what they had been taught, but what was missing was the understanding they had to watch the other aircraft and fit the procedure they were taught into the practical situation of flying safely, such as by following the leader, in this example. I thought, *There has to be a better way to do this.*

Seeking Solutions

This situation stayed in my mind and started the wheels of innovation turning. I knew there had to be a more efficient way to teach, and obviously, we had to find a common ground between instructor and student. We developed different methods to help prepare students to learn in a simulator before they got in the aircraft and how to adjust our way of teaching to give more guidance. We adjusted our way of teaching by introducing the idea of following the sequence of traffic as well as the procedure. This was a great way to prepare us all before we went in the aircraft. It still played in the back of my mind that pretraining instruction would be helpful. And the idea began to form: *why not move to the university in Beijing, China, where the students were coming from, and teach the students prior to them coming abroad?* After several months of communication with the university, I secured a job to start teaching at the university in Beijing in September 2007.

With the goal set, and knowing I would be wrapping up my life in Canada for a while, I ruminated on starting my new adventure. I thought about how I was going to teach the students, who had no idea what to expect. But I realized there was a pattern to my experience, and this would be the basis of my teaching. I wanted the students to learn about having direction, like *a dream*. There were obstacles that would have to be overcome, but these obstacles would help to establish their desire to keep working. Working hard includes self-awareness, repetition of knowledge, and strategies to remember. And finally, it's important to *keep your mindset positive* even when the situation is discouraging, as this is the only way to not give up. When I first started teaching in Beijing, I had to practice perseverance, as shown in the following example.

My first class was daunting for me—well actually, the first couple of months were. I felt a bit insecure about how to teach and get the ever-important information from my brain to the students' brains in a way that they could use it practically when they went abroad. The students were very forgiving and kind, and they probably didn't even understand how at a loss I felt, some days planning my lesson on the way to class. What makes teaching a class daunting for me is that the students have certain expectations, and without formal teacher training, I was sure I would fall short of these expectations. I only had a flight instructor rating, which required four months of training, training I had done on my various jobs. I did not have the typical four to six years that academic teachers receive.

But I plunged forward with energy and enthusiasm because that is why I had turned my life as I knew it upside down: I had a message to deliver, and it was worth all that to be here and deliver my message. Now, I am delivering the same message in this book: how you as a student or trainee can follow a framework of motivation, obstacle surviving, steps of hard work, and a perseverance mindset. This method is basically all the lessons I've learned in my life put into a framework that applies to any learning situation, whether it be at a new job or while preparing for your chosen industry. I hope you enjoy this practical guide to acing any learning situation in any learning environment! From my experience, the mistakes I've made, and the lessons I've learned, I want to extend the pattern and framework of coping with life as you strive to accomplish your dream. In writing this book, this is my pledge to you, and I hope this book will be invaluable in enhancing your life!

Before we get into the framework and how to apply it to your own situation, the next chapter will cover the human aspect of learning, being trained, and how to cope with these necessary facets.

Chapter Summary:

- Find your dream by looking at your childhood interests and strengths.
- Seek advice from people you trust.
- Research your chosen field for education and skill requirements.
- Accept obstacles must be overcome.

FUTURE

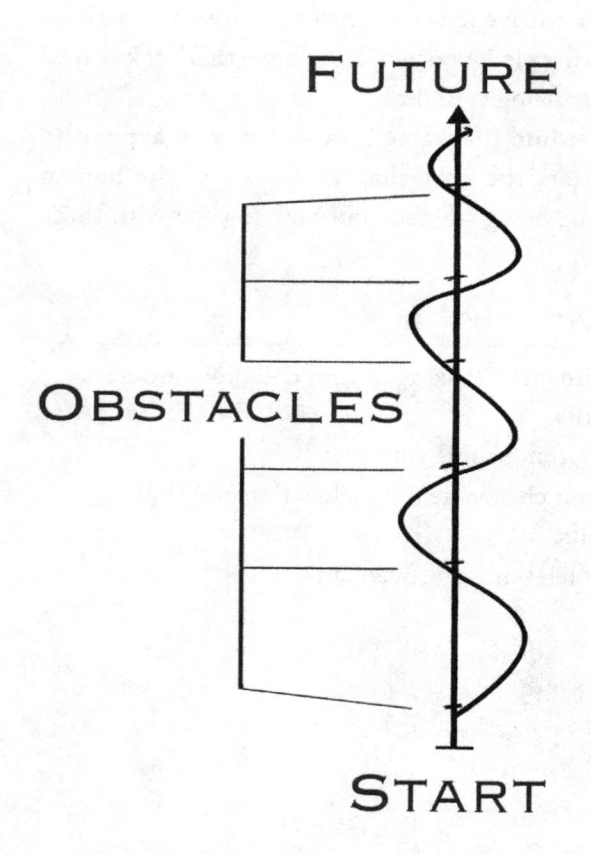

OBSTACLES

START

CHAPTER 2

A STRONG FOUNDATION:

THE WHY AND DEFINING SUCCESS

WHY? SUCCESS!

Two Pillars of Strength

You have made your big decision, and now you stand on the verge of an adventure of a lifetime that will change you, mold you, and make you a better person all around—just like I was standing in the classroom in Beijing, China, looking into the faces of my students, knowing I had committed to a challenge and that I would see it through, although I did not know all it would entail. So, you are now at the starting line, and in making the decision to do this, you have committed to a challenge that will reward you for the rest of your life. The first step of your learning journey is to set the initial foundation pieces: your motivation for learning this specific topic. Why are you here? There are so many different motivations for getting an education, moving to a new job, or starting a business. Maybe it's a practical financial need, a desire for status, or a dream from childhood, or maybe you just want to try it because it seems challenging. The point is to think about why you are here, why you made this decision, and lock it in. This is your motivation that will keep you going when the going gets tough. We all have reasons for why we make our choices, and they aren't right or wrong. The reasons are yours and only need to be important to you. So, keep them close and remind yourself of them whenever you are feeling overwhelmed with the training and learning.

When I teach my classes, at the start of the course, I ask my students two questions:

1. Why do you want to be a pilot?
2. What is your definition of success?

These two questions are a good way to get my students to speak English and become comfortable with expressing themselves in front of a stranger. But the deeper meaning, for me, is to start them thinking about their end goal and their motivation for this challenge. If you know why you want to be a pilot, and you really think about it, it will become one of the pillars in your foundation of a solid education. When you think of success, you are looking to the end game. If you don't know your goal, how will you know when you reach it?

So, now that the parameters are set, you can ask yourself, *Why am I on this journey? And how will I know when I've reached the destination?*

For the "visualists" among us, think of these two questions as the base for the bridge of learning. Your answer to the *why* question is the starting point and the foundation under your feet now. Answering the second question gives you the foundation on the other side of the chasm, where you will place your feet after this learning journey!

Accepting Life as a Human

Now that the basic, foundational questions have been answered, let's start to build more support. There are a few more premises to understand when setting to the task of acquiring knowledge and becoming what you have committed to become. As we live life, there are challenges we all have to face, and how we deal with these challenges makes a difference in the outcome, both for ourselves and for the people around us. Emotions are universal. Sometimes people ignore them and hope they go away, but that doesn't mean they don't react to them. The people in our everyday orbit—like coworkers, friends, and loved ones—are left to deal with the fallout from us not recognizing and dealing with our reactions to situations or events. This can cause problems in a working or learning environment.

I like to think about where each person starts—the "fiber" of their thoughts, so to speak. The mental environment is molded and influenced by many things, but it starts in our childhood—where we grew up, our home life, our friends, and how we were treated and thought of. I'm not a psychologist, but I have learned that this is what makes us all a bit different. This influence on our thoughts can become a barrier to our learning, or we can learn to use it to our advantage. There are several ways to become aware of what "makes you tick," or how you process and organize information in your mind. This will be covered more in chapter eight.

Personality and Learning

The first step is to do a personality test, like I did in my guidance counselor's office. By doing so, you can discover your strengths and weaknesses. Usually, we know about ourselves because we live in our head twenty-four hours a day, seven days a week, but during our childhood and teens, we need guidance and validation. I was fortunate to have a guidance counselor who listened to me. A quick note here: weaknesses aren't something to be ashamed of, as we all have them and learn to accommodate them in our lives. Always remember that perfection is an illusion; striving for it is essential, but it won't be attained 100 percent of the time. Working on improving your weaknesses is a lifelong task, but when you get discouraged, find a way to use a strength to get yourself back into the groove again and refresh your confidence so you can dive into the task.

Once you have finished your personality test, you can do a learning styles test as well. I like to think of learning as having two parts: hearing and receiving the information and then storing it so you can recall it easily. There are basically three types of learning and storing knowledge: auditory (hearing it), visual (seeing it), and kinesthetic (doing it). This is useful information to know because it helps you take notes and get the information in a way you will remember, which in turn helps you recall it. Once you have these types figured out, you will be better prepared to organize your information on paper and in your mind. This is the start of awareness and aligning yourself for the intake of information specifically for your mind. For access to personality and learning style tests, you can use a counselor, as I did, or search for the many resources on the internet. There are many options, but they will all basically give you an idea of what direction to start with. Using the results from these tests and thinking about what your unique strengths and weaknesses are will set you up to learn efficiently and gain the ability to do targeted learning.

The External Environment

Moving halfway around the world to start a new life is not the typical way to launch a career, and the environment was an adjustment. What I observed very quickly was that I was the minority, and I was in a country that had its own way of operating before I ever set foot on the streets. I was a guest in this culture, and I wanted to conduct myself as such.

A person's living environment and work environment are different but influence each other. For example, I had to budget my time to get to work better than I had to in Canada, because in Beijing, I had a ten-minute walk as opposed to a twenty-minute drive, the difference being I couldn't speed as easily on my feet as I could in a car. Also, the clothes I wore to work were different. Walking to work in freezing temperatures instead of driving a car with a good heater made a difference as well. All these tiny adjustments were just that, tiny, but they had to be made a part of my life, and if the adjustments weren't made, I suffered the consequences.

A life skill that I didn't take too seriously in Canada was food prep and eating at regular hours. I never kept a strict schedule and only ate when I was hungry. In Beijing, I was on a strict schedule, and I found I got really tired if I didn't eat regularly. My students were very good at eating their meals on time, so that helped me get into the routine. A surprising fact that came up was that all the talking I did while teaching made me very, very hungry. I always felt I wasn't expending a lot of energy, so I wouldn't need much food, but your jaw and brain are working double time, which adds up!

Learning to Adjust

To apply this to the student or trainee life, adjusting to the lifestyle of being a student is important, and these adjustments might be major or minor depending on what stage you are at in your life when you start training. It is important to consider these life adjustments and be ready for them.

The major part of the environment that will affect your training is the relationship between you and your instructor. This relationship and adjusting to it is not something that is usually considered. The student is taken up with the new goal, the chance to realize a dream and the practical allowances that must be made. The student-instructor relationship can be the making or breaking of your learning experience, and awareness is the first step. It is so important and must be dealt with in a delicate manner.

Every industry has a hierarchy. Because of this, training on the job becomes the learning environment regardless of how long the training period is. If a person goes to university, there are at least three to four years of training, and they expect to be in the "receiving knowledge" seat. This seems to be forgotten in a work training environment, and expectations for performance can be unrealistic. Every job in the world has an adjustment period; the "new guy" has less knowledge than the rest of the team, and all the feelings of being a student are still there, though maybe not as obvious. This doesn't mean they should be ignored or that the trainee can't take some control of their training and set themselves up for better success. We can't control people's behavior, but we can prepare ourselves. This framework will help you to have a little control, even in a work training environment.

In the aviation industry, for example, pilots need an instructor rating to teach. These pilots may be young and have just finished with their own training. Don't let this worry you!

Their youth is not a reflection of their knowledge; they meet all the qualifications required to teach a person how to fly. With youth, their life experience is not as high, but they know how to fly an aircraft and keep you safe. The instructors are also growing and learning. While their flight skills may be very good, they may not have the best communication skills, and this is where you as the student will need to help the learning process. Remember, being forewarned is being forearmed!

With all these things said, any instructor will do their job and teach you how to fly. It is a vitally important relationship and should be cultivated to get the most out of the experience. As a student, you can't be expected to know the information prior to studying it, but you will be expected to do the reading assignments, practice activities, and studying to be prepared for the next lesson or flight. You must bring your A game, as it is said, because this is what you control. I'll give you some tips on how to deal with the other more uncomfortable aspects of a less-than-ideal instructor-student relationship later, in chapter five.

Just like me, when I was standing in the classroom wondering how I would do this monumental task ahead of me, you will have the same feeling when you start ground school as a pilot, sit in your first lecture in university, or start your first day in training at a new company. There is a lot of information to learn from a variety of subjects. These subjects layer together and can be cross-referenced with different situations and concepts, depending on previous knowledge. Getting the proper foundation is vitally important, and having a step by-step, logical process is the best way to tackle this situation. I like to tell my students to be at least 51 percent excited and less than 49 percent nervous; this allows the excitement to give you the momentum to get over the first day!

An example of this in aviation is needing to know about biology and how the body functions so you will know what to expect when you are flying at high altitudes. You must know about physics so you understand how the aircraft flies. You will learn about communication to use the radio, as well as task organization and prioritization by using checklists. I describe a pilot as "a person who needs to know a little bit about a lot of topics." You need operational knowledge about a lot of topics so you can deal with any problems that may happen.

Another example could be a production line. If you observe your trainer and how they place their hands and feet as they work in their station, this will be a good indication of what you should do from a safety perspective. The trainer may not think to tell you this information, but it is something they do without thinking, so observing is very important, as well as listening to what they do say.

Internal Environment

The last point about the environment the student should be aware of is the mental environment, or the mindset you have. Mindset is a powerful thing when it is used in the right way. In my opinion, there are two basic ways of looking at life: negatively or positively. This basic rule is applied to any situation, and most people have a default attitude they use. To give you a real-life example, my father is a gentleman and a very good father. I don't remember him getting angry with us as children. He would deal with our mistakes and problems with patience while looking for the solution or how we could move on and learn from the issue. To me, this is a positive way of dealing with life. On the other hand, there are people who will always see the negative or what can go wrong with a situation. This is not always a bad thing, but if it interferes with a project moving forward, pushing yourself to achieve your goals, or starting something new, this can be a real problem. There are very few people who like being in a position of feeling less than or dumb. Learning and training puts you in a position of not knowing, so these feelings are very close to the surface. Each of us deals with these feelings in a slightly different way, but it does make us feel more vulnerable, and therefore, we can be more sensitive. It is easy to take comments and actions personally when we are vulnerable, and then we can get into a negative spiral. It will take a great effort and lots of positive internal dialogue to stay positive and move toward the goal. However, you won't stay in that vulnerable or "not knowing" position forever; you will learn, progress, and build confidence. This is just a transition point in your learning, so muscle through and succeed!

The one thing to remember as you read this book is that being a student takes a lot of grit and determination. This is a big task and has lots of moving parts, but it is so worth the journey. You will become a different person and should be proud of your accomplishments but humble enough to acknowledge your humanity. You will become a person who develops skills, becomes a professional, and becomes ready to serve in your new opportunity.

The next chapter will cover the framework I developed from my personal story, struggles, and learning. This framework will assist anyone starting a new career, project, or job, or simply growing from a situation. I call this the ACE the RISK™ wheel. The visual is in the shape of a wheel, and it has you as the individual in the middle, the ACE as the rubber, or outside, and the middle as all the areas you will have to cope with in the new venture—the RISK portions. Now that you have your feet firmly on the ground, let's dive into learning the framework!

Chapter Summary:

- Build the foundations by knowing your why and definition of success.
- Find your personality type and learning style.
- Accept your humanity in both strengths and weaknesses.
- Observe as well as listen to your teacher and trainer.
- Bring a positive and overcomer attitude, especially at the beginning.

CHAPTER 3

ACE THE RISK™ WHEEL:
FRAMEWORK FOR SUCCESS

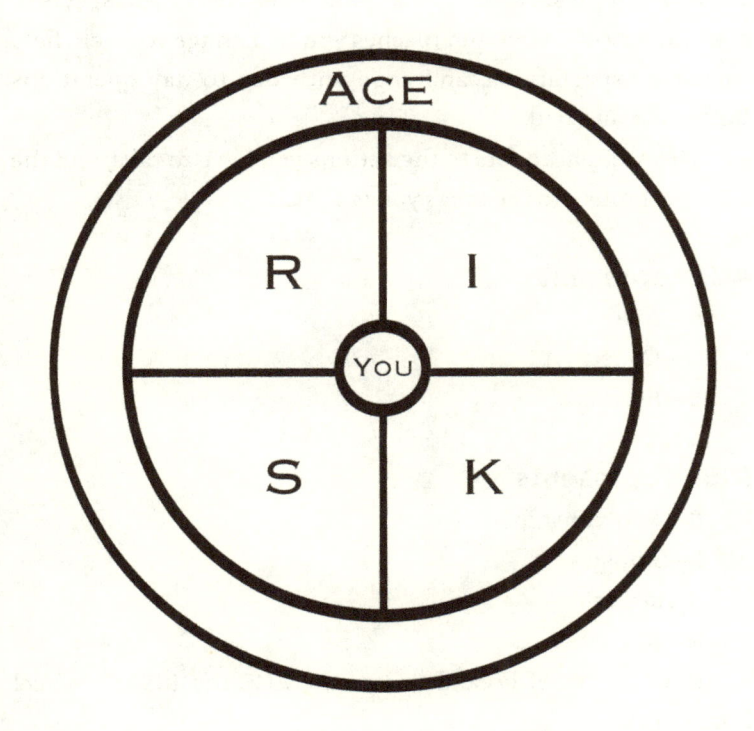

```
         ACE
      R  |  I
         YOU
      S  |  K
```

When I was teaching in China, I can thankfully say I didn't stand in the classroom every day wondering how I was going to teach the students this knowledge. I started to formulate a plan to teach the information in a logical and building-block manner so the students could understand and build on it with their own organization methods. Eventually, the ACE the RISK™ wheel framework was the strategy I developed based on the patterns I saw in my own experience, as well as the students I was instructing. It started out as a visual to organize material and ensure all topics were covered over the semester. But as I spoke with friends and family who were both training and receiving training, I realized this method could be expanded to any training or learning situation. This framework covers all aspects of the industry of choice and teaches you to manage yourself, field industry expectations, and cope with day-to-day operations, both good and bad.

The ACE part refers to the actions you have to take, and the RISK part refers to the areas you will ACE.

ACE represents
    A – Assess
    C – Construct
    E – Evaluate

RISK represents
    R – Relationships
    I – Industry
    S – Situations
    K – Keynotes

Here is a brief breakdown of the ACE the RISK™ wheel framework.

Assess—A
Assessing is taking the time to step back and look at each and every thing that comes across your path. You want to look at a situation, event, or exchange with an open mind, not only from your personal perspective. The goal is to look at things in

a balanced and objective manner, not with a reactive and emotional response. If you reduce the emotional aspect of reaction, then you can look at facts and make better choices.

Construct—C

Constructing is how you are going to build a solution for a situation, event, or exchange. After assessing the event, you can then construct a way to respond and proactively solve the problem. With the assessment and constructed method to deal with the event, the stress involved is reduced and more control is given to the outcome.

Evaluate—E

Evaluating is the final action step. Evaluating is ensuring the assessment and construction of the game plan to deal with the issue actually works. If the plan isn't working, this is the stage to make adjustments to the constructed plan.

ACE are the action steps, and they can be repeated at any stage when the learner or trainee doesn't feel comfortable with an outcome or the result is just not working as expected.

Now let's look at the RISK section; these topics are basically the "fixed" variables.

Relationships—R

Relationships are how you as an individual will interact with your work environment, your fellow workers and managers, and yourself in this new environment. It is important to know what to expect so you can be prepared and have an appropriate expectation of and reaction to these relationships. This is where you set boundaries and plan actions if relationships aren't working out.

Industry—I
Industry involves several aspects: the purpose of the specific industry and the standards within that industry. Attitudes and nuances that result from each industry are more subtle and harder to define but still need to be considered.

Situations—S
Situations can be divided into normal, abnormal, and extreme circumstances. These are situations that arise in every job regardless of what it is. Normal operations will happen most of the time, abnormal some of the time, and emergencies hopefully happen very rarely.

Keynotes—K
Keynotes are how all the aforementioned topics apply to you as an individual and how you will fit into your role in the industry. The keynotes are unique to each person and should be used as a tool to help you thrive in your career and in your life.

The first semester I was in Beijing teaching, I taught mostly general English classes and only had a couple of aviation-related classes. I found this overwhelming at first because I didn't really know where to start with the lessons. What helped me was being in a foreign country myself. What language skills did I need for everyday living? From there, I started to teach my students in English what I needed to know in Mandarin. It made perfect sense. As we touched on in chapter two, being a student or in the "not knowing" position isn't easy. Practically speaking, it is frustrating trying to communicate, and on a self-confidence level, it can wear down your confidence quickly. Additionally, it is lonely, because we don't want to be embarrassed, so we tend to shut down. For these reasons, this framework was developed, to reduce that chance of being embarrassed, losing confidence, and shutting down.

The ACE part of the framework contains the actions. Every section of the RISK part has ACE applied to it, and examples will be given in depth in the following chapters, using the aviation industry as the basis. There are a couple of points to remember for the ACE section: if something dramatic happens in your training or learning situation, you will have emotions to deal with. Emotions are very natural, and you should feel them. I would like to advise, however, that you not do an assessment while your emotions are running high. This can lead to assuming the worst about someone's intentions when they didn't mean what you thought. Communicate with the people involved, seek advice from someone you trust, and let yourself feel the emotions first, then deal with the problem.

Constructing is straightforward and will be covered in the examples in context. **Evaluating** is the aspect of ACE that is on the individual's time. If you have an analytical mind, you can evaluate the results of the assessment and construct. Some situations will require all three to happen close together, while others will occur over a period of time. For example, if you are having trouble with a colleague, you can't just resign, so this evaluation takes place over a longer period of time as you interact with that colleague. If you go through periods of not seeing the colleague often, then the evaluation takes longer. If you work with said colleague every day for eight to twelve hours, then assessing, constructing, and evaluating happen every day and sometimes almost at the same time.

There's a final point to the ACE part. Why are we even doing the action steps? The reason we are doing these steps is twofold. First, you will be better prepared for day-to-day activities and ready to cope with tasks and interactions, as well as keep your confidence. The second reason is for you as the trainee, student, or new employee to set your boundary—not a boundary for quitting but a boundary of when you have to step up and ask questions, get more information, and take control of your own training. If an individual doesn't take control of themselves and let their trainer or instructor know what they need, opportunities can be lost.

The RISK part breaks down the big topics in any industry and gives guidance on how to build tools, ways of coping, and efficient learning techniques to remove stress from your learning or training experience. There are some industries that will focus on one topic more than others, and each training situation won't go into great depth, but the topics can still be considered. The goal of the framework is to prepare you for what to expect and forearm you with knowledge so you can be ready to deal with most eventualities, which will result in less stress.

So, welcome to the first steps in your very rewarding career in your chosen industry! You are starting on a spectacular path, and you will succeed, making it so worth the hard work! We have established your motivation and when you will reach success. We've talked about how to find personality and learning style tests and how helpful they are for preparing for your learning journey. We have even looked at the ACE the RISK™ framework and what it means. But how does all this information help you? That is the next section. We will go into more detail on how to apply this framework, using the aviation industry as an example!

Chapter Summary:

- Assess the situation.
- Construct a plan.
- Evaluate the success of the plan.
- Understand necessary relationships.
- Apply these concepts to relationships in the industry, the industry environment, day-to-day situations, and keynotes (the unique individual application).

CHAPTER 4

ACE THE RISK™ WHEEL, APPLIED TO AVIATION

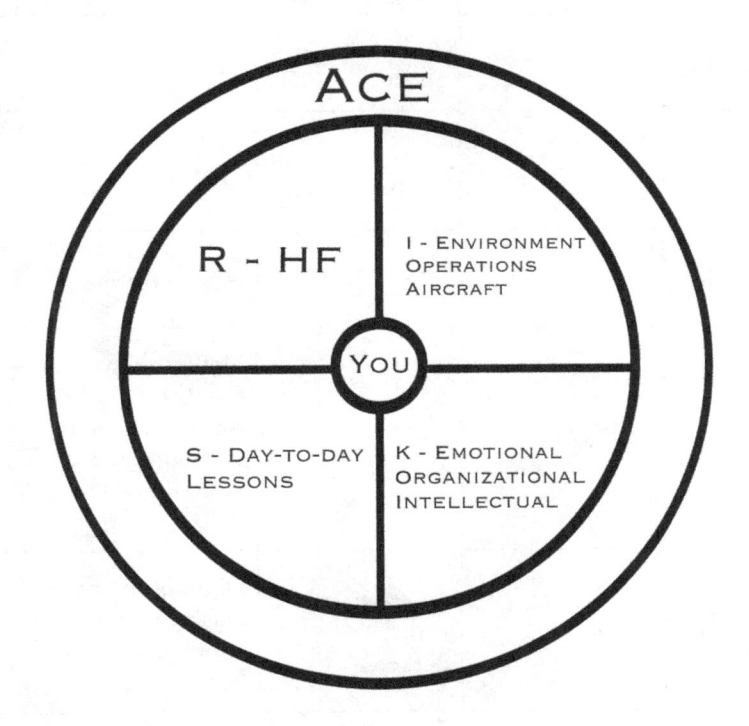

```
            ACE

      R - HF      I - ENVIRONMENT
                  OPERATIONS
                  AIRCRAFT

             YOU

      S - DAY-TO-DAY   K - EMOTIONAL
      LESSONS          ORGANIZATIONAL
                       INTELLECTUAL
```

The ACE the RISK™ wheel is a framework I developed to give an overview of the subjects to cover, the big picture, so to speak. This is a way of organizing the topics in basic groups by association to start putting the materials into patterns so you as the student will remember information better. The visual of the wheel is set up so that you, the student, are the center. Each section is between you at the center and the outside circle, which is made up of the action items, ACE—basically, how you as the pilot deal with all the topics in a flight or training event.

The ACE the RISK™ wheel has five large groups, with topics in each one:

Topic	Basic Framework	Aviation Application	Aviation-Specific Topics
You	YOU	You as pilot in command (PIC)	
ACE	ASSESS CONSTRUCT EVALUATE	Same but for an aviation context	
R	RELATIONSHIPS	Human elements	Human factors
I	INDUSTRY	Environment Operations Aircraft	Meteorology (weather) Navigation, radio communication, ATC Aircraft systems, theory of flight
S	SITUATIONS	Day-to-day tasks Lessons	Flight preparation and closing duties Flight skills for each lesson
K	KEYNOTES	Emotional skills Organizational skills Multitasking Intellectual skills	Patience, tenacity, disappointment Lists, graphics, note-taking Prioritizing, memory/recall techniques Situational awareness, decision-making, basic communication

PIC—Pilot in Command

The PIC (pilot in command) is *you*, the student pilot at the center of the wheel! Your unique and individual characteristics must be understood to streamline the acquisition of knowledge so you can recall it quickly.

As I stated earlier, doing a personality test and learning styles test and answering why you'd want to be a pilot and what success means to you are all aspects of the preparation associated with the PIC section of the ACE the RISK™ wheel, as you learn everything and how it relates to you. These basics were covered in the first three chapters.

R—You

You (R) includes human factors, a course taught in flight school, which involves the psychological, physiological, and emotional aspects of being a human and how they relate to operating an aircraft safely. We learn how our body and mind work and react in normal situations and emergency situations so we know how to "manage" the body when we are in those situations. The human body has limitations, just like a machine does. We can push ourselves to our limits, but at some point, we will break down. As a pilot, it is important to know those limits and respect them. That is why this course is very important when becoming a pilot.

I—Environment

Environment (I) is a complex topic about meteorological phenomena. For a pilot, this topic is extensive, as it directly affects the aircraft and will cause changes to flight paths and the comfort of the flight, as well as cause damage to the aircraft if severe enough. The meteorology course in flight training includes how weather develops, how it is reported to pilots, and how to avoid or cope with a weather situation that is not ideal.

I—Operations

Operations (I) covers the internal environment of the aircraft and the external environment of airspace. Inside the aircraft, the student learns how to operate the different levers and buttons. We have checklists and standard operation procedures (SOP) that make these tasks easier because there is a definite sequence of operations. The outside environment is not in the pilot's control; they have to follow instructions and sometimes react to another pilot's actions. This environment has many rules, which will produce expected behaviors, and is the focus of another course covered in flight training.

I—Aircraft

Aircraft (I) is obviously a vital part of flight training; this is the whole reason a person decides to be a pilot—so they can fly an aircraft. The aircraft has many parts, systems, and maneuvers it can do. In-aircraft flight training systematically covers all the maneuvers that could happen in the aircraft so the pilot is well-trained for any possibility. This training will continue yearly for the rest of the pilot's career.

S—Situations

Situations (S) are the day-to-day flights, lessons, and classes the student attends. As stated, each maneuver is taught and practiced in the aircraft, so these situations will require slightly different preparation and theory to review. This is good practice to build on previous flights, develop the big picture of the theory, and improve reaction skills in case of an event when they are needed.

K—Keynotes

Keynotes (K) come back to the individual. They are the skills that are developed behind the scenes while you are learning hands-on skills. These skills are unique to you, and you will develop them without recognizing them at first. These skills are multitasking, situational awareness, and such—thinking skills.

This is the aviation breakdown of the RISK part of the ACE the RISK™ wheel. The ACE part is done in every section before a class or flight or when the student is studying. Each flight you go on, you will use a combination of all the topics in the ACE the RISK™ wheel. Here are examples displaying the connections between theory and procedure while preparing for a flight:

1. Preflight inspection (walk-around)
   - Check oil and fuel quantity—linked to aircraft systems theory
   - Check structure of aircraft—linked to theory of flight

2. Weight and balance calculation
   - Linked to theory of flight
   - Linked to flight operations theory

3. Takeoff and landing calculation
   - Linked to aircraft performance theory
   - Linked to flight operations theory

The first time you step into your chosen flight training facility, you are entering the world of aviation. Here, you will learn structure, guidelines, rules, and parameters you will stay within and follow to become and remain a competent and safe pilot. That makes it sound very daunting, and maybe a little scary, but I assure you, with patience and hard work, you will get there. We've learned so far to start with the basic foundation of your learning journey: *Why do I want to be a pilot, and what is my definition of success?*

Once you have these two questions answered, you will have your motivation for learning and your goal for where you are going and be able to recognize it when you get there.

The foundations are established. Now the main supports will be analyzed. Find out about yourself and how to use your unique individual learning method to store and recall information. This can be found using online tests that will help you become familiar with yourself. Also, look at your childhood and try to remember what ambitions you had then and what ideas and dreams have stayed with you throughout school; this is a good indicator of your memory patterns and internal desires.

Once you know yourself a bit better, and you've made the decision to become a pilot, the next step is to get a medical examination from an aviation-approved doctor. This is a crucial part of becoming a pilot! After the medical examination is passed, it's time to enroll in a flight training program; this can be at a college, at a flying club, or with a freelance instructor. After researching the possible programs for you, then it is time to enroll and get excited about starting training.

Ready, set, go!

Chapter Summary:

How the ACE the RISK™ wheel applies to aviation:
- Relationships: YOU—human factors and how you relate to your body, yourself, and the industry.
- Industry: the expectations from operations, aircraft, and the environment.
- Situations: day-to-day tasks and objectives to be learned and covered.
- Keynotes: how all the above information applies to you and how you can acquire and apply it.

CHAPTER 5

R—RELATIONSHIPS:
HOW YOU FIT IN YOUR WORLD

As stated in earlier chapters, relationships are super important in any work environment. Even if your job is quite solitary, at some point, you will deal with someone. Learning to manage these relationships will make your day-to-day life at work easier and more enjoyable. A disclaimer here: there are some people who just refuse to be gotten along with. When you have tried your best and they just aren't going to cooperate, you will have to make a decision on what is best for you and your life. You can keep fighting, give up, or remove yourself from the situation. Whatever you choose to do, the relationship with yourself should be the top priority. The following is a breakdown of relationships and how they are viewed in the aviation world.

Psychological
This includes learning attitudes, dealing with stress, decision-making, and dealing with emergencies. Learning attitudes are a problem when they become a barrier to getting the information you need to reach your goal. In chapter two, we covered that it is reasonable to think that people don't like being in a place of not knowing, which is exactly where a student is. In this particular situation, we as humans can react in different ways, and it's

usually a subconscious reaction. For your benefit as a student, be aware of how you react so you can get rid of the barriers. This, again, is about you managing yourself, your emotions, and your learning journey. You can take charge and organize yourself.

Physiological

This subject will take you back to high school biology. You will be reminded of certain body systems and how they act and react, and then how they react differently because you are at thirty thousand feet. The best way to understand how your body works differently in flight is to think of it as a compromised environment. You still have air in its typical composition, but the quantity is less than on the ground, so there is less O_2 available at high altitudes. As we know, oxygen is essential to our bodies, and it affects every bodily system. When we fly at a high altitude for long periods, our bodies may react differently, and it will be surprising which systems will be affected. When you understand what can happen, you learn how to deal with it and what to do to minimize the associated risks.

Emotional Aspects

These aspects are a little trickier. We all react differently to the same stimulus; dealing with this is very much the student pilot's responsibility. We live with ourselves every day and have an ongoing conversation with ourselves; therefore, we know ourselves the best. We learn to live comfortably with ourselves. All of this is to say that some days we will be in a more sensitive mood, some days less sensitive, and if we have a confrontation, we will act differently. Keep in the foremost part of your mind that we can't control people, only ourselves, and if they are rude, mean, etc. (especially an instructor to a student), you will have to manage yourself and your reaction so learning can continue.

I had a student once who had a great personality. However, I am easygoing and not forceful as an instructor. My teaching mentality is that the student wants to learn, and I'll be beside them to guide them to learn what they need. I will not be a source of motivation by berating, being angry, or demeaning. The learning environment was not suitable for this particular student due to my teaching style, because he needed more pressure. We could be friends but not student and instructor. I asked my supervisor to give him a different instructor because I wasn't the right one for him. He was assigned another instructor and finished the course with all his licenses. Know yourself and know what's working for you and what's not working for you. Again, you don't get to choose who you will fly with, so learn how to adapt and manage your emotions to reach the end goal. Learn how to play the long game!

Your Instructor and You

Let's talk a little more about instructors, as they will be an integral part of your training throughout your career. We can self-study a lot of theory and information, but thankfully, we can't get in an aircraft or a simulator and self-teach ourselves. So, instructors are needed to go with us, to keep us safe while we learn from their expertise to fly an aircraft. An instructor is a brave individual who should be recognized and honored for the job they do, but that doesn't mean you will click with every instructor. As mentioned earlier, they are also human and still developing in their careers and lives. This relationship is essential at the start of your career development, and you will use people skills from the beginning. Now, why does the student need to use people skills?

There are several reasons. In a learning and teaching situation, the student puts themself in a place they are unfamiliar with, and this causes apprehension and a feeling of being "stupid." The point is that you as the student don't know the information, that's why you're there to learn. This situation makes the student a little more sensitive, often making them take things personally. It is also very likely you will have more than one instructor throughout your training, perhaps even up to six or seven. Learn as much as you can from each instructor, as they all know the basics, but you as the student will click with some instructors better than others. This is where you will need to use people skills to achieve your goal of learning. When you are licensed and flying commercially, you have no choice in who you fly with, so learning to get along with all types of people as early as possible is recommended.

The instructor may be young, even younger than you, but don't worry, they have done the training, practiced teaching with a senior instructor, and passed the test, so they will be very qualified. They will sit beside you in the aircraft, so they have to keep you safe to keep themselves safe. You could have a patient, understanding instructor who gives constructive and proper feedback, or you could have an instructor who puts in the bare minimum and just fills the seat as an instructor. In this latter situation, you have to do your part in acquiring the knowledge and feedback you need to improve your learning experience. Here are two important points to remember: you can only control yourself, not your instructor, and you are here to learn how to fly, not be "buddies" with your instructor.

If you have an instructor who is understanding and who can see your needs and meet them, then you are fortunate. Not all instructors are good at communicating or teaching. There will be some who don't mind making you feel dumb, and others will always be taking the controls so they can fly instead of letting you practice. Whether you have a self-centered instructor or one who is concerned with your progress, you are going to have to find the confidence to move beyond their behavior and keep working on your skills. This is part of your training, because in every industry, there are people like that, and sometimes they become trainers. Stay strong and keep pushing for your goals; you won't be in training forever. Even with a good instructor, you will typically have times when you are confused, don't understand the point of the lesson, or have questions. An instructor can have anywhere from three to ten students who all have different challenges. This work is hard and requires a lot of energy, so understand your instructors may be tired and stressed.

As a student, you can help yourself immensely by learning how to ask questions in the best way to get the information you need. For example, let's say you have landed from a flight and finished up the tasks required to secure the aircraft. This is your sixth flight, and you are having trouble getting the touchdown just right. Your instructor tells you it was a great flight but has scored you a two out of four on your landing (two meaning "needs more work"). You want some constructive feedback, but your instructor has another flight. So, you can ask the instructor how you can improve your landings by getting them to describe the technique and procedure again. This helps a busy instructor by asking a specific question and helps you by focusing on one task per flight to improve on. The key is to not ask the question in anger or with a bad attitude; ask it by genuinely inquiring for your improvement.

Make a Plan

Try to make your own plan for what skills you want to focus on and how you want to improve on each flight instead of leaving it all to your instructor. They will guide you, but you can set a high standard for yourself. You will receive an outline of training, so use this to make a rough plan. Take some control of your own training. You don't know the information, but you can take the lead in getting this knowledge when you know your style of learning and recall methods, which helps your instructor and yourself! I'm not saying you should tell the instructor how to teach the flight, but from your knowledge of yourself and how you learn, you can make a list of goals for yourself that fit in with the instructor's plan. For example, if I am at the stage of training where I am learning different landings and takeoffs, I have about twenty hours of flight training, and this stage includes four flights, each about an hour and focused on one specific type of landing and takeoff (crosswind, soft/rough field, short field). For my first specialty type of landing and takeoff lesson, I would focus on the specialty type, plus set a goal of perfecting my circuit or traffic pattern a little more each flight.

For the first lesson, focus on making the circuit nice and square to the runway. In the next lesson, focus on keeping the altitude correct at each stage. And for the third lesson, focus on maintaining airspeed on approach. If during these three lessons, you focus on three different things to try and make them as perfect as possible, then on the next flight, these three skills should be more natural.

It's important to not only ask the questions but to ask in a way that will get an answer without emotions getting involved. Don't let your frustration rise until you are angry; deal with the situation right away. If you allow yourself to get angry and start asking questions, the response will likely be angry as well. Two angry people don't get very far, and your progress will be stalled. As in relationships and situations in life, it is best practice to deal with an issue right away and ask the questions you need to so you can further your education or learn where you can adjust. Keep it about knowledge of the subject of the lesson or flight. Each lesson, the instructor will have expectations of you as the student; they require you to have prepared and done the reading for the lesson, done any review or preview activities assigned, and be in the attitude of wanting to learn and improve your skills.

Don't get personal and don't take it personally if the instructor is not the most pleasant. Remember, they have the answers you need. In the industry, you will likely have a cranky captain you will fly with, so learn how to be professional early on. These basic skills of self-management now in your toolbox provide the largest foundation for your learning journey and career. Now, we'll get into the overview of the learning process to become a pilot.

Back in the classroom in Beijing, standing in front of the class at the beginning of the course, everyone was eager—at least more eager than at the end of class, especially before lunch! Teaching about aircraft was always a little tricky, as systems are best learned in the contextual process of how they work. There are a variety of systems to talk about as well as theory, including basic physics, which needs to be taught in sequence and correctly. I really didn't want the students' eyes to glaze over, leaving me standing at the front of the class talking to myself, because we had lost the plot in some system.

As I would start the class with attendance after the bell, I would ask my first question: "What is the most important part of the aircraft?" The students answered with various responses:

the wings, the engine, the navigation equipment, etc. The answer I was looking for was the pilot! The aircraft won't move or be useful unless the pilot is in it, hence the pilot being the most important part. Although I view the pilot as the most important "part" of the aircraft to make it operate, the aircraft itself is the second most important. The relationship between the pilot and the aircraft is vital to understand and manage. We have to understand our aircraft and how it works; we don't want to be afraid of it, because this can be counterproductive. If we understand how the aircraft flies through the air, it will help us develop the skill to act and react correctly so we don't make a situation worse or put ourselves in an undesirable flight maneuver. The same mindset works for systems; we want to respond correctly to help the situation, not make it worse.

Understanding Your Role

First, understanding that the pilot must control and manage the aircraft sets the precedent that the aircraft is a tool to be used. You fly the aircraft; don't let it "fly" you. How can an aircraft fly you? Remember, once that aircraft leaves the ground, there are no brakes until you are back on the ground, so there is no stopping to think or figure it out midair. This is why ground preparation and studying are essential to making the most of your flights. You want to know what to expect and what is expected of you in your role of controlling the aircraft. If you understand your role in this "relationship," it makes being in control easier. On the part of the student, reaction time will be slow at first, but you have an instructor there to help with that. As you learn and progress, you will react quicker, and more correctly, until it becomes second nature to you. At this point, you have a skill!

In chapter six, we will learn more about our aircraft, the industry, and the expectations that come with the industry as we cover the *I* in the ACE the RISK™ wheel. You will learn about the new world you are entering and how to navigate that world.

Chapter Summary:

- Psychological, physiological, and emotional aspects and how to deal with them.
- Understanding your relationship with your instructor and planning to deal with them.
- Remembering your motivation.
- Understanding your role and where you fit into the industry and learning process.

CHAPTER 6

I—INDUSTRY:

THE WORLD YOU ARE ENTERING

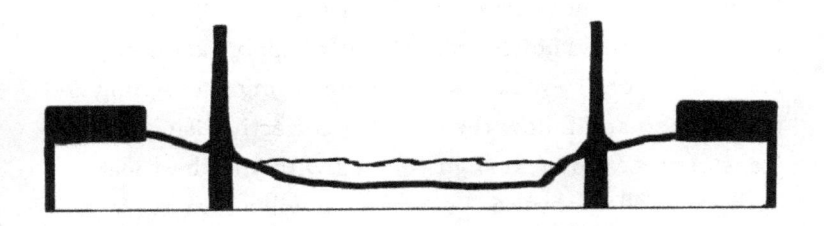

Industry Hierarchy

After the basic self-learning/awareness aspects have been recognized and figured out, it's time to look at you and your chosen industry. Each industry has a certain hierarchy of employees, a certain code of ethics or expectations, and a reputation as a whole. The industry I'm familiar with, the aviation industry, is very dynamic, both physically and metaphorically. We are always moving people and products to places. But it is also an industry that ebbs and flows with world events, as most recently observed during the pandemic. This career is very rewarding, but it also requires the people who are part of it to be adaptable, resilient, and problem-solvers. These are skills you will develop as you learn, work, and gain experience in the industry. But before we get established, we have to go through the learning process. Next, we will cover the foundational information and aspects to be aware of before you start the journey. We've talked about yourself, your body, and your mental environment, now let's talk about the physical environment: the cockpit, the meteorological environment, and the requirements of air traffic control are all part of the environment section of the ACE the RISK™ wheel.

The knowledge required to become a pilot covers many topics that overlap, so there seems to be a lot of information, and it can be overwhelming in the beginning. A pilot needs to learn a lot of topics but not necessarily be an expert in all of them. We need operational knowledge, or "how to apply" knowledge, of many situations so we know when something goes wrong and can respond and follow the checklist correctly. Using the first steps in this chapter to align yourself with your best learning path, you will start to see patterns that will allow you to organize and understand the overlapping info, where and when to use certain tools, and how to get to the desired result. The information is layered because of how the industry is structured.

Pilot License Sequence

Medical—PPL—night—CPL— (instructor) —multi—IFR (instructor)—ATPL

After you have decided that being a pilot is your destiny, the first practical step is to complete an aviation medical exam. Transport Canada is the governing body for the aviation industry in Canada, and each country has a similar agency. This agency makes the air laws, does investigations and audits, and provides standards and resources to help people in the aviation industry. On the Transport Canada website, there is a list of approved aviation doctors who can do your medical examination for whichever region you live in. This medical examination is done according to the medical requirements and standards deemed by Transport Canada.

Once the medical exam is passed, you can find a school where you can learn how to fly. There are several types of courses you can take, which are offered at different schools across Canada.

University Degree: This option is offered at flight colleges across the country. It is typically a four-year program that will provide you with your licenses (private pilot license, night rating, commercial pilot license, multi-engine rating, and instrument rating) and a degree from a university in partnership with the flight college. This is the most expensive.

Aviation Diploma: This option is also offered at flight colleges. It is typically a two-year program that provides all licenses (private pilot license, night rating, commercial pilot license, multi-engine rating, and instrument rating) and a diploma received at the end, with the additional courses coming from a community college associated with the flying college. It's not as expensive as the degree.

ICPC Certificate: This is a one-year program that delivers all the licenses (private pilot license, night rating, commercial pilot license, multi-engine rating, and instrument rating) and is presented in a logical structure to be completed in a year minimum, depending on weather. This is the second least expensive option. The flight school I chose to go to offers several options: ICPC, diploma, and university degree programs. When I attended the school, the university degree program wasn't offered, as it was added later.
In the above courses, it is assumed the student will be a full-time student.

Modular Learning: This type of course is done at the pace of the student and when the time can be allowed for training. This course is available at most flying clubs and flight colleges and is pay-as-you-go.

Once you have chosen a program that fits your needs, time commitment, and financial capability, you are free to start your training. Ground school and flight lessons typically start simultaneously in Canada, while for modular programs, either one can be started first, but there is a time limit that the other one has to be completed by. (This is in Canada, but other countries may have different course timelines and availability.)

The beginning of training will include some safety tests to ensure you are ready for basic flying. You'll do a PSTAR exam (in Canada) to get a student pilot permit, a FTOM (flight training operations manual) exam to learn the operations of the specific school, a POH (pilot operating handbook) exam to learn the systems and procedures of the aircraft you will fly, and finally, you will have to do a radio course and exam so you can get a restricted radio license (from Innovation, Science and Economic Development Canada), which is required to use the radio in the aircraft.

With all that learning and testing done, you are on your way to a PPL (private pilot license). This is the first license achieved in the college programs. There is a recreational pilot license that can be achieved, but they are usually done at flying clubs and for pilots who fly for a hobby, not a career.

Flight Hours Timeline

(These are average hours for Canadian licenses, and it varies for each student.)

0 hr	15 hr	45 hr		150 hr	165 hr	200 hr
	1st solo	PPL		Multi-Engine	IFR	CPL

PPL (45 hours of training)—Upon completion, you will have a license to fly an aircraft but not to make an income.

Night rating (need a PPL)—Will allow you to fly at night.

CPL (need a PPL plus 65 hours of training for a total of 200 flight hours)—Upon completion, you will have a license to fly commercially and the ability to make an income with your license.

Multi-engine rating (need a PPL)—Allows you to fly an aircraft with two or more engines.

Instrument rating (need a PPL)—Allows you to fly in clouds and bad weather to a certain limit.

ATPL (requires a CPL, multi-rating, IFR, and 1500 hours of total time)—Allows you to fly as an airline captain.

Instructor rating (need a CPL) —Allows you to teach flight and make an income doing so.

The above hour requirements are based on the minimums provided by Transport Canada. If a student pilot needs more time, that is okay. During your training, there will be times when you feel way behind your classmates—the weather has not cooperated, you haven't flown in several weeks, and you feel discouraged. Always remember, the bad weather will end, you will overcome the obstacles, and you will thrive again. View this as a competition with yourself, not your classmates. Every student will struggle with certain things, and progress ebbs and flows. Achieving the skill to the point it is second nature is the most important. As a career pilot, transporting people will be your future; they need to trust you, and therefore, you need to be a competent pilot and trustworthy, so spend the time and effort to become just that!

As shown on the timeline, the first ten to fifteen hours of flying is pre-solo, and your instructor will do everything in the very beginning. On the first flight, the instructor does the flight prep and all flying as a demonstration to the student. After that flight, you will be expected to start taking over more and more tasks with each flight. It will be a gradual transition, but you will be given tasks right away. The best way to prepare for this transition is to watch what your instructor is doing. The first ten hours, you will likely feel very overwhelmed because everything is new, and you know you will have to eventually do this all yourself. This is true, but at this point, take it one lesson at a time and try to be a sponge—absorb everything you can. After the flight, go home and mentally review the flight lesson, then do the reading and activities assigned for the next flight. Try to find the link between the lessons and the knowledge, as this will build your foundation of flight knowledge and therefore your skills.

Environment—Weather

The larger environment that you will operate in is the actual atmosphere and weather that happens in this atmosphere. Inside the airplane, we have a lot of control over what, when, and how things happen, but we have no control over the outside environment. We must learn how to read the signs and then adapt and react to what the weather is doing. For example, on the east coast of Canada, the weather can be temperamental, and we have a fair amount of snow in the winter. One day, I was up with one of my students in the training area doing our lesson, knowing snow was forecast to hit the area where we were. Since the weather is unpredictable, instructors always keep a good eye on what the clouds and precipitation are doing so we can return to the airport quickly if needed. Several of the instructors went up flying and had an opportunity to get one last lesson in before the snow was supposed to start. We were in the training area teaching the lesson, and the snow started to come in before it was forecast. We all returned to the airport so we didn't get caught in the snowstorm. The benefit of flying is you have a great view of the weather that is coming in. We were all watching the west, where the snowstorm was coming from, and we reacted by returning and landing safely in enough time. When bad weather is coming into an area, you have to be more alert, be aware of consequences, and react in the safest way. There are a couple of things I always remember about weather: never trust the forecast, because it is as accurate as possible but can change without notice, and never panic when something happens. Instead, take a deep breath, make the best decision for the situation, and don't take chances with the weather, because it is so unpredictable.

When you are learning the theory of weather in ground school, it is a large subject with many facets. When trying to grasp the basics of meteorology, remember you have already learned the basics of weather in elementary and junior high school. When we were kids and going through school, we often asked, "Why do I have to learn this?" This is why! Here are some basic elementary school principles we learned that are practical in aviation. State changes, from liquid to solid to gas and vice versa, are the foundational aspect of weather. We also learned about how heat is created and distributed across the globe, how the atmosphere characteristics change depending on how far we go from the Earth's surface, and the relationship between the Earth and the sun at different times of year. All these basic concepts affect how weather is developed and the situations created that a pilot will deal with during a flight. Meteorology theory is basically a chain of events that happen in a certain order and with different influences. Once you start to grasp these concepts and understand different scenarios, or chains of reaction, you will learn the actions a pilot will take that are appropriate to the situation.

So take courage. Meteorology is a large topic but a manageable one with these tips about the order of events and the knowledge you have learned previously. We have talked about your own individual environment where you learn and the physical environment over which we have no control but will learn the correct reactions for, and now we will go over aspects of "operations".

Operations—ATC

We have learned about our internal mental environment and the fact that we have to be aware of it and manage it. We have also learned about the atmosphere and how we react to that environment. Now we will learn about the regulated environment of airspace. Aviation has been around for just over one hundred years. A lot of lessons have been learned over the years, and regulations and rules have been established due to these lessons. The aviation industry includes the whole world, which makes it quite unique because it means rules have to be the same in many countries and streamlined so it is easier to fly between countries. Can you imagine flying to a different country and needing to learn all the air laws for that country just for one flight? Over the evolution of aviation, ICAO was established to cope with this need for universal guidelines. ICAO, the International Civil Aviation Organization, is an organization under the United Nations umbrella that makes suggestions and mandates based on investigations and conclusions from groups of aviation professionals from different countries. This organization provides guidance and then each country builds programs and laws so that international flight is much more streamlined and feasible around the world.

ICAO set a mandate that each pilot in the world who flies into international airports needs to pass an English language test focused on radio communication and aviation-specific language. This was mandated in 2008 and has since been implemented throughout the countries that are part of ICAO. This test came into being because miscommunication was found to be a part of the problem in many accidents and incidents. Together, this mandate for language and all the other air laws give us a structured airspace.

Canadian airspace and the way to conduct aircraft in this environment is very clear-cut, and Transport Canada has rules to govern behavior in airspace based on the direction of ICAO. These rules make it easier to learn, although it seems like a lot in the beginning. Airspace is divided into different levels of control, and there are rules to decide altitudes for flying, which dictates where and how we fly. These rules are easy to learn because they don't change; you learn them, you follow them, and everything is very predictable. This aspect of the environment can be studied and learned on the ground before the flight. I recommend this method of pre-learning; the more prep you can do on the ground, the better it is for you during your flight. You will be flying the plane, listening to your instructor, trying to learn, and talking on the radio, so pre-learning is essential. It will help you to eventually get the sequence of actions and the priority of tasks, and the skills will become concrete in your mind.

The airspace is divided vertically, with different types of flying permitted in each section, such as VFR (visual flight rules) and IFR (instrument flight rules). For example, VFR requires you to have a minimum of three statute miles for visibility. IFR is for flying in clouds, and to land and take off, you need half a mile as a minimum. There are three kinds of airspace surrounding airports. A busy airport with a lot of aircraft will have a controller who tells pilots what to do. A less busy airport has a person to talk to who gives information but doesn't tell the pilots what to do. Finally, there are airports that have no person to talk to, which are called uncontrolled airports, where the pilots talk to one another, follow the procedures, and adjust their path to accommodate safety for all involved. Later in the book, this communication will be covered with more explanation on the types of airspace, but it is a key link to be mentioned here. There are certain procedures for flying in controlled airspace, but also for delivering and receiving information in a structured manner, that each pilot learns and follows so everyone in the industry is basically on the same page and will have the same actions/reactions to clearances, instructions, and requests. It is by working together to follow the rules that everyone is kept safe and able to complete flights efficiently.

We've talked about ourselves and our mental "environment" and our physical environment inside and outside the aircraft. Now let's talk about the equipment we use as pilots. What does this involve?

Aircraft Systems

One of the easy things about the systems of the aircraft and how they work is that they are like math; if you input the numbers and follow the formula, you will get a predicted answer. A system in the aircraft will do the same. For example, if I increase the power lever, the aircraft will go faster. If it doesn't, we have a procedure to deal with that situation.

Keep in mind that you will learn the limitations of both the minimums and maximums of the aircraft and its systems. These are important to remember! If you keep the aircraft in between these limitations, you are in the normal range and will produce predictable results, like the math equation. There are different procedures for breaking a maximum limitation and for breaking a minimum limitation.

Learning an aircraft system can be overwhelming, as it includes a lot of detail. The following method is one I developed to break down each system of the aircraft for ease of learning/remembering:

The P-Logic™ System
- The purpose of the system
- The parts of the system
- The process of the system
- The problems that may happen with the system

The aircraft is like a car; to ensure correct operation, there are systems that work together to make the vehicle move. These systems include an electrical system, a fuel system, and an oil system, to name a few. These systems each follow a process that must work in the designed order or there will be a failure and therefore an emergency. Each system on the aircraft has a specific <u>purpose</u>; if that purpose is understood, it leads to understanding how the other three parts work together. The parts and process work together because you need the parts to fulfill the process of the system, which then allows the system to serve its purpose. It helps to keep the parts with the right system if you learn in this sequence. Problems have specific indicators that show the pilot the system isn't working correctly; in other words, the purpose of the system isn't being achieved, and your job as the pilot is to deal with this until you can land and hand it off to the maintenance engineer to have it fixed.

Let's look at a normal training flight and how the oil system works during this flight. We'll look at the oil system working normally and how, if something breaks, the pilot deals with the emergency. There are predictable emergencies with any type of aircraft, but the aircraft manufacturer and operators of the aircraft develop procedures to deal with emergencies based on the manufacturer's operating handbook and the experiences of the operators. The following example is a basic, generic emergency to illustrate the use of the P-Logic™ system.

- Oil system: piston engine
- Purpose: lubricates, seals, cleans, cools
- Parts: oil sump (pump), oil cooler, oil filler/cap, reservoir
- Process: Oil is held in the reservoir (engine off). The engine starts, and oil moves through the lines thanks to an engine-driven pump to the crankshaft and splashes around to lubricate. As oil gets heated from the friction of the metal parts, it is sent to the cooler, where the oil is cooled, and then sent back to the sump.
 This system needs pressure within the system to operate effectively.

- Problem 1: low pressure, caused by a leak in the system, means you are losing oil.
- Problem 2: high oil temperature, caused by an engine running too hot, means there's not enough oil in the system, and there is an oil leak.

Emergency procedures will provide the actions to take in each situation, which are covered later in the book!

This method is a very structured way to learn a system and associate it with the checklist. The purpose of all the information a pilot absorbs is to provide functional knowledge, or operational knowledge, not knowledge in great depth. As a pilot, we don't have to fix the system that breaks; that is the maintenance engineer's job once we get on the ground. The pilot has to understand how the system operates and what can go wrong so they can operate the aircraft safely and without making the problem worse until they get to the ground. In the oil example, there is no way I as a pilot can get out and open the engine compartment to check for an oil leak. But I can operate the aircraft at a lower power setting and get on the ground as soon as possible so the expert can fix it. I keep the engine at a lower power setting to help keep it cooler, and I land as soon as possible so I'm not flying for prolonged periods with a disabled engine.

If you learn a system alongside the normal and emergency procedures/checklists, this will help you remember the procedure in context. After verbal review and memorization, sitting in the aircraft, and creating muscle memory with the procedure, the system will become second nature during your flights.

Now we are going to apply this mentality to aerodynamic theory, or the physics of flying an aircraft. On a personal note, I found physics a hard subject to grasp. This was probably because I did it online and it was very self-directed. I'm a visual learner, and I like to see how things work in order to understand them. Learning physics from a textbook was rather mind-boggling, but I made it through and passed so I could go to flight school. When I started to learn theory of flight, or physics, I started to go into the mindset of *I don't get it; I'll never understand this*.... But what I slowly realized was that it actually made sense as I applied it to the procedure and what my instructor was trying to teach me in the aircraft. Context made all the difference! Fast-forward to Beijing, China, where I was teaching the basics of theory to students. Imagine my shock that I was describing it all in physics terms! I really was surprised and finally understood that *context* is the key to understanding.

Here's a simple breakdown of flight theory: The aircraft has aerodynamic limitations, just like each system has its limitations. If you go less than the minimum aerodynamic limit, you don't have enough lift to sustain flight, meaning you stall the aircraft. If you go over the maximum aerodynamic limit, you have several problems: you overstress the airframe and any maneuver will overload the designed G-load of the wings. Neither of these situations is something you want to deal with on a flight. If these limitations are exceeded, your job as the pilot is now more difficult, and the stress level has increased on both you as the pilot and the aircraft as a structure.

Context and Limitations

I strongly suggest you take the theory of flight and study it with the procedures in your personal study. A key to understanding and memorizing the procedures is to remember you are keeping yourself within the normal limitations, or the safe zone. We learn the extremes with our instructor in a safe area so, as pilots, we recognize the signs and recover before we get to the extreme situation. As already stated in this book, aviation is a little different than other industries. We teach the extreme limits so we know you can handle these situations when you fly solo. Ideally, you never want to get into these situations, but if you do, you'll be able to read the signs, do the correct recovery procedure, and get back to normal flight. This will become second nature, or a built-in skill. Then you will be thinking like a pilot!

When you start training, you learn normal flight first and the indications for that flight: wing level, cruise attitude in relation to the horizon, etc. Then we teach low-speed situations, flying near the low aerodynamic limit of the aircraft. These maneuvers are called slow flight, a stall, and a spin. If slow flight isn't recovered, you will stall, and if a stall isn't corrected, you will spin. These maneuvers are not taught to scare a student but so you will recognize the situation and know how to recover correctly and quickly. These lessons are all done in the first ten to twelve hours.

About 90 precent of your career flying will be done in the normal range. We spend a lot of training time on emergencies to keep the skills sharp but spend most of our time flying in normal phases of flight. The saying in the aviation industry is "Plan for the worst and hope for the best," so this is our mentality!

A Word of Encouragement

Don't be afraid of learning these maneuvers. It doesn't feel comfortable, and you may feel a little ill after you practice them, but that is good because you know you don't want to be in that situation. All those feelings will be an indication you are in a situation you don't want to be in, and this will help you recover.

You are the most important part of the aircraft, so you have to take and be in control. Make the aircraft do what you want it to do!

So, how do all these individual items of knowledge and information fit together to make you a better pilot and employee? This will all be tied together in the next chapter, which talks about navigation and situations. There, you will have an opportunity to link all the knowledge and put it in the correct context.

You now know why we learn the limitations of the aircraft and why we practice flying close to the limits: so we can recognize and recover. We've talked about airspace, the environment, and procedures to operate in this environment. And we talked about the 5 percent of flying that we must learn for safety. Now let's talk about the 95 percent of flying you will do. As stated earlier, we will spend most of our time in the cruise attitude, climbing, descending, takeoff, and landing—normal phases of flight. And we will not just practice maneuvers for an hour and then come back to the same airport. Eventually, we are going to go to another airport, like going on an adventure.

Operations—Navigation

The next topic we'll cover is the broad topic of navigation. There are several sections under navigation, including types of planning. Starting out as a zero-hour pilot, you will learn how to plan with a plotter, map, marker, and planning sheet. You will learn this process in great detail in ground school and practice it for every cross-country flight you do in your training. There are software programs that can do it for you, but on the written exam, you will have to do it manually, so it has to be taught and practiced manually. There is another reason for learning the manual way: if you know and understand the planning on a foundational level, you will be able to catch mistakes more easily when you review and approve the electronic versions. Again, practicing the manual calculations will instill this knowledge in your mind so it becomes second nature and identifying errors is done quickly. Remember: practice makes knowledge become a skill, which then becomes second nature. This is the goal of training, not perfection!

There is a flow to doing the calculations, and you need a lot of information from several places. Use your planning sheet as your guide to what information you need. For VFR navigation planning, you plot on the map the track you'll follow on the flight and the drift lines (lines from the departure airport that are 10° on either side of your direct track in case you get off track). These drift lines are drawn from the departure airport and destination airport so if you get off track, you can calculate the degrees off and how to get back on track. Getting off track and continuing off the track can result in a miscalculation in fuel, which can become an emergency situation if it isn't corrected. Then you choose checkpoints (features on the ground that you use to ensure you are on the right path and also within the timeline you predicted in your planning). This is confirmed by calculations you do during your flight, checkpoint to checkpoint. Checkpoints are typically between ten and twenty nautical miles apart, but your instructor will guide you on this point. The plotting on the map can be done the night before your flight. When you do this is basically decided by you, but earlier is better.

The day of, about an hour and a half before your flight, you will do the rest of the planning using the most up-to-date weather reports and forecasts possible. This planning will include the METAR/TAF, weather reports, and forecasts for the departure and destination airports. You will do some calculations to determine density altitude and pressure altitude. These numbers will then be used with the performance charts in the POH of the aircraft you are using. These charts, with the weather calculations, will help you determine the fuel and time required for the flight, as well as the power setting for the flight.

With all this information, you can go back to your map and calculate estimated times to each checkpoint with distance, time, and landmarks. These calculations give you a forecast of where you should be and when. It's similar to creating your own checklist but using landmarks as items to check off.

Reality of Planning

There is one note of caution I want to give you here: don't panic if the planning and the actual flight don't match up! During all my training and teaching, there was only one flight that worked out to be exactly the same as my planning, and that was a night flight with very calm winds. It is okay if it's off a little. If there are extreme differences, make sure you planned it correctly so the next flight is accurate. It's important to find major errors before you learn a skill incorrectly, and your instructor can help you with these questions.

Flight planning for VFR flights is a bit tedious and time-consuming, but again, you are learning the basics of navigation, and if you pay attention, you will learn what looks right and what looks wrong in calculations. Then, when you get to IFR planning, or electronic planning, you can very quickly catch mistakes.

Here are a couple of tips on doing VFR navigation planning, or manual planning:

1. Draw your lines on the map, which can be done ahead of time.
2. Fill in the planning sheet with the following:
   - Info from map
   - Info from METAR, or aviation weather report
   - Calculations from whiz wheel/electronic flight computer
   - Info from POH performance charts

Navigation brings many pieces of information you have learned together, and this is when you start exercising your pilot skills. The final step is to look at each flight. Whether it be a navigation or cross-country flight, or a flight lesson on reaching the aerodynamic limits of the aircraft, it should be viewed as a situation or an opportunity to exercise several specific skill sets you have been learning and developing.

Operations—Radio Communication

Radio communication is a unique skill that pilots and air traffic controllers need to have and will use every flight. When using the radio, you can't rely on body language or nonverbal cues to understand the messages exchanged, so you will rely on listening comprehension and verbal skills. Standardized language has been developed to help reduce errors in radio communication within the aviation industry. ICAO, which we discussed previously, comes up again when learning about the universal language of aviation. In the early to mid-1900s, English-speaking countries were active in the design, development, and production of aircraft and the growing aviation industry. Due to this fact, English was chosen as the international language for aviation, with certain words requiring specific actions and responses from pilots. The organization that now calls itself ICAO met in 1944 and decided on mandates, one being the official aviation language of English. In 2008, ICAO set in place criteria that have to be met by each country to test pilots' English language ability. This is to maintain a certain level of English for every pilot and controller who has to operate in or with international flights.

ICAO gave the directive for each country to make its own English testing system, but radiotelephony, or standardized language, is only part of the communication. A key point here: every radio communication must have a response. If the pilot talks, ATC will respond. If ATC gives an instruction, clearance, or information, it has to be acknowledged by the pilot. A lack of two-way communication indicates a problem, and the emergency protocol will be initiated by ATC. Communication will be covered in a later chapter in greater detail.

The topics that have been covered thus far are the specific ideas and knowledge needed for the aviation industry. In other words, just like a doctor needs to learn medical-specific information, a pilot has to learn aviation-specific information. This will be relatively new, though some parts may be more familiar. As stated earlier, a pilot needs to know a little about a lot of topics. Some you will be strong in, others you will work hard to attain. The theory is directly related to procedures, checklists, and step-by-step training that can be learned, memorized, and tested easily. However, there is another set of skills that are harder to define and identify but equally important; these will be covered in the next section.

Chapter Summary:

- Industry hierarchy and a general timeline of learning to be a pilot show the expectations.
- Weather/meteorology is a large subject, so break it down into basic principles you have already learned previously.
- Airspace is bound by rules for safety, making it easier to learn and predict behavior.
- You must learn the maximums and minimums of aircraft systems.
- P-Logic™ is the way to remember the systems of the aircraft.
- Planning in navigation will not be exactly what you fly, due to slight changes in weather, but proper planning is always required.
- Radio communication is essential in aviation.
- Listening properly and doing the correct action are important parts of communication.

CHAPTER 7

S—SITUATIONS:

DAY-TO-DAY TASKS AND LESSONS

The next step to developing yourself into the pilot you want to become is to look internally and find the resources you already possess. You will learn and strengthen skills of the trade, but you already possess strengths and raw talent, as each person is born with individual and unique strengths and weaknesses. The strengths and weaknesses you possess are the reason any training you receive will be custom to you. Recognizing and accepting this is key to developing into a master of your own story and becoming an elite professional in your industry.

There are several assumptions and ground rules that must be established before we go into this stage of professional development. First and foremost, you must understand there is no such thing as perfection. We all have faults and will all fail at times. Some days just won't go well, and that's normal. Striving for perfection is good motivation, but understand that this will not be achieved each and every time. There will be times you will do things perfectly, and that is a fabulous feeling—very good for confidence building. But there will also be times when you don't do everything perfectly. Use these situations to improve your skills. Failure is not a be-all and end-all. It is uncomfortable, and you can allow yourself to feel it for a while, but then analyze it and use it to rise higher. Becoming a pilot, as we've already established, requires hard work, repetition, and perseverance.

EQ versus IQ

The secret to thriving in life, whether in a training environment, a university environment, or even in regular everyday relationships and interactions, is understanding the value of being "right" but doing it in the right way. As an instructor, I can tell my student they had a very bad flight and get angry with them. I am right, and as part of my role as the flight instructor, it can be perceived as my "right" to tell them that. But will it actually be an effective way to help them progress as a student? No, it won't; it will feed my ego, but that's all it will do. That kind of behavior creates barriers, not pathways to greatness. The difference between correcting in a manner of arrogance and correcting in a manner of growth has to do with EQ. EQ is emotional quotient, as opposed to IQ, which is intelligence quotient. As a society, we focus on and have a variety of tests for IQ, which makes it easier to measure. But really, EQ is what sets someone apart as an effective instructor or an exceptional human being. Knowing the information is good, but knowing how to apply it to each student's personality is what makes it effective. Flight instructors are not trained to be teachers through getting a degree; they are taught how to fly well and how to give you the basic info you need to learn. They are there to keep you safe and allow you the time and space to learn. If you have an instructor who understands how to apply the knowledge to your way of learning, you are very fortunate. But if you don't, don't despair, there are ways you can help yourself. The way you ask questions can give you more info than you would typically get. The underlying rule for me, which I instill in my students, is to learn how to cooperate with your instructor. This will develop your EQ as a student, and it will help you in your career. You will not get to choose the captain you fly with, so it is best to manage yourself and learn to adapt to the situation. A pilot's life is about adapting to any situation and maintaining professionalism. It isn't always fair, and it doesn't always make sense, but the point is you are learning and getting what you need. The training will end, so don't let a poor instructor stand in your way to success!

We have talked about the structure and standards of the industry; they are unbending and must be followed. Now it's time to look at and develop a structure of behavior within your internal environment: your brain, emotions, and spirit. These intangible skills, or soft skills, are just as important and necessary as practical aviation skills. The difference is that each pilot has to make these skills their own, and measuring these skills is not as cut-and-dry as touching down at one thousand feet down the runway. Having this knowledge of yourself will make the theory and aviation-specific information become part of you as a pilot. This part of the journey is unique to you and is more ambiguous than the theory of flight, radio communication, etc.

The key to making the best of any situation, especially your training, is your attitude. You and you alone know yourself the best. It's important to accept there is no perfect person or someone who does everything right; we all have strengths and weaknesses, and this means you should only compare yourself to yourself. In every situation in your training, look at the good, the okay, and the not-so-good so you can focus on that and improve. If you don't look at each situation with this attitude, it can become a barrier to learning and achieving your dream.

You must realize these skills and attributes are developed

over time. It may take ten attempts doing a takeoff to get it just right and make it second nature, but the internal skills will seize and develop long term. These skills are developed over a career, but being aware of them early on will lead to mastering them earlier. This is all part of the process of becoming a mature and balanced professional in your field.

Finally, these skills often develop in the background. While it's obvious to focus on controlling the aircraft, listening to the instructor, and seeing the progress in these tasks, it isn't easy to see patience develop or that you are more situationally aware than you were at the beginning. These skills are harder to recognize when they are developing because it is not as obvious as your hands on the control column. It is essential you are aware of the need for them, but also be ready to see them in yourself so you know when you're reaching your goal. It helps to have someone who can be objective and will let you know when they see certain skills developing. Also, create benchmarks for yourself, and when you reach them, reflect on how far you've come in the journey, of both your career and your life. I don't want you to get the idea you have to be all sentimental and sensitive, but you do have to be practical and honest with yourself. Dream to stay motivated; keep it real to develop!

Lessons

All pilot training includes flight operations. This course combines many of the separate items of theory. This gives many pieces of information in a situational context. This course reviews a lot of information that has been learned previously but in a functional timeline and practical scenarios.

How do all these topics and knowledge fit together and layer into each other to teach us how to fly, become competent pilots, and thrive in this industry? The best way to show this blending (collaboration) is by looking at situations, which give the information in context. Everything you learn will be in a situation, or a specific context. Each piece of theory must be learned and understood individually, then these pieces need to be put into the standard situations so you can understand how it all works together. For me, if I understand the why of a checklist and procedure, I will remember the knowledge point or procedure.

For example, the definition of a stall is insufficient airflow over the wing to sustain flight due to reaching the critical angle of attack. The solution is to increase the airflow over the wing. Makes complete sense, so how does the recovery procedure reflect that?

For the stall recovery procedure, the first two steps are as follows:

1. Pitch forward
2. Add full power

Putting the nose down lessens the angle of attack and increases the airflow over the wing, which increases the amount of lift. Adding full power allows the airflow to increase in speed because it's making the aircraft fly faster. These two actions reestablish straight and level flight. Learning theory in context, like with this example, will help you start connecting the dots and make it easier to acquire the skills you are learning.

I will caution you here: try not to micromanage the information, meaning don't learn it in a vacuum or compartmentalize it. You will have to apply it in situations, so the sooner you learn it in context, the easier it will be for you later in your education.

In the beginning, the information will be broken down into smaller pieces, but as you learn more and get deeper into the topics, you should be able to start making connections, which will give context.

The provider of your training will also have a structure in which the knowledge is presented. For example, you will have a lesson plan every time you fly, even for a solo flight. This will list the things you need to do and practice and any specific issues you may have to work on. Communication with the instructor is important before, during (if a dual flight), and after the flight. Ask questions or for an item to be redemonstrated if you're unsure of the requirements, and let them know what you think you need work on. This indicates to the instructor you are paying attention to your own training, are aware of your limitations, and are trying to improve.

When I was taking my entry-level instructor training, I enjoyed the ground school and learned a lot. There was only one thing that threw me off a little. We had one person who would tell us precisely what we should do and give the information in a step-by-step way, but then there was another person who would tell us stories and present the information in an offhand way, with very little precision. I personally found this very confusing and wasn't sure what to follow because there was such a huge difference. I ended up failing my flight test, and part of it was due to the little demon of doubt in the back of my head always saying to me, *But which one is right?* I stopped flying for a month and went home to try to figure out what was wrong. I reflected on the fact that the more precise instructor was the one to listen to because he backed up what he said. I went back to the flight school, did the test again, and passed because I didn't listen to the doubt and knew I was doing the right thing.

Remember, the goal of each flight is to keep the aircraft in the normal range for each phase of flight (lessons to learn the procedures if outside these parameters are exempted). Learning about the systems, limitations, and what to do to keep within these limitations will ensure you stay in the normal range, and this will build your confidence as you keep working toward your goal.

This is a journey of self-discovery to become what you desire, and part of that process is learning to have a healthy relationship with yourself. To do this, we will break down the intangible skills required to know yourself and how to use this internal picture to develop yourself and your career so you can become the ace you want to be!

Chapter Summary:

- Perfection is a goal to strive for but won't be attained all the time.
- You have a unique set of strengths and weaknesses, use them to customize your training.
- Compare yourself to yourself.
- Have a good attitude; improve yourself.

CHAPTER 8

K—KEYNOTES:

MAKING THE JOB YOUR OWN

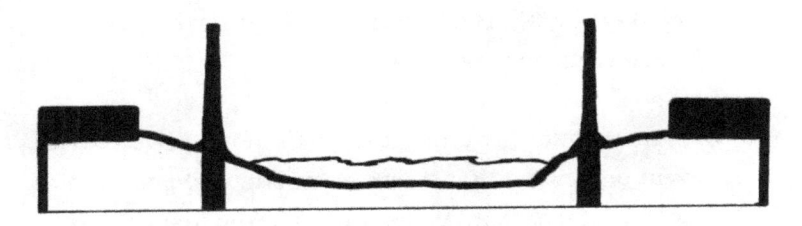

If you learn how to hone these next skills, they will set you apart as a high-level pilot or employee. These skills, being harder to identify, are the deeper skills, or the soft/intangible skills. They are associated with our personalities and character. The key is being aware of them and making a conscious effort to improve them. This will give you the "grit" factor when things get tough in training, as well as in your career. There will be times when it's tough, but this is when these skills will be exercised and very useful. These soft skills will be developed as you build basic flying skills. These skills are like the programs running in the background when you use a computer, except you are the computer in this case.

Ground Rules

First and foremost, you don't have to have a certain personality or be a certain type of person to be a pilot. The key that will unlock this door is understanding you will need patience, perseverance, and hard work to succeed. To understand the world within ourselves, we have to have a look at what is required by the outside world. Here are a couple of general life rules that must be navigated to become successful:

1. There isn't an easy, fast solution to achieving success.
2. The process, or journey, is necessary to make the knowledge or skills your own.
3. Forgiving yourself is necessary for long-term success.
4. Never give up on moving forward.

With these four rules understood, let's move forward. With every event or incident that crosses our path, we have a choice of how we will react to it. As mentioned in the first chapter of this book, we decide if we will react positively or negatively, which in turn makes things more difficult or tolerable. If we accept that life isn't going to be easy, we will be ready to take it one step at a time and be more willing to solve a problem or obstacle instead of giving up immediately.

We'll use working toward a private pilot license as our example (refer to page 56). Within the first twelve to twenty hours of training, a student pilot should go solo. For the first solo flight, the student does one circuit: a takeoff, the circuit or traffic pattern, and a landing. This is a major confidence-building flight, and there are a lot of skills that have to be achieved in a short period of time for the instructor to feel comfortable enough to allow the student to do this solo. This is exactly why a solo flight is a requirement for a private license to be issued; it proves to the student they can do it and the instructor has seen evidence the student can do it.

If a student reaches around ten hours and they aren't close to going solo, they start to panic and feel stressed. We tend to compare ourselves to the group we are in and use that as our standard of where we should be. In any group of students or people, there will be ones who are faster at some things and others who are slower. We can't let that frustrate us, demotivate us, or discourage us. We have obstacles to overcome in our lives, and we can allow them to either stunt or fertilize our growth. Yes, being faster is desirable, but if you aren't, settle down and pick apart the flights and see how you can improve yourself. If we allow the fact that we are slower stunt our progress, it will become a vicious cycle. Our emotions will take over, we won't be able to get past that feeling of despair, we'll get more and more discouraged, and it will frustrate our efforts while also generating more and more stress. Basically, this starts a downward spiral of emotions that can throw us off track completely.

Patience

Exercising patience in this circumstance is key. Patience is simply giving yourself another chance to do better. But when you give yourself another chance, take the time to analyze the last lesson, see where you are having trouble, and find solutions to that issue. Ask your instructor, ask your friends if they are experiencing the same thing, and do some searching on the internet. I will caution you on using the internet, though. The internet is a good resource but not always a credible source. So always use the flight school and instructor as the authority, with the internet being supplemental. The internet is a good resource, but you have to learn according to your flight training program. Use the internet with discretion and to assist with what your instructor will tell you. Don't use it as an argumentative tool to disagree with your instructor; this will make for an uncomfortable environment, and you will sabotage your own learning. Experience is really the best teacher, and there are instructors who have a desire to share their experience with students. My desire for you as the reader is to use my experience to help you be an excellent student and build tools to make you a respected professional. You can see more on my website: *languagenavigator.com*.

So, patience allows you to give yourself more time to work out the issues. Remember, every problem has a solution. Patience gives you the time and space to figure out the problems, then you need tenacity to keep going. After you have had a discouraging flight lesson, you have to "get back on the horse," so to speak. Go back and start again—though you're not actually starting again, you are starting from your last experience. If the last flight didn't go well, you know what *not* to do on the next one. Forward progress is excellent even if it's a small step. I used to tell my students, "If you want to perform poorly at English, do nothing!" The same advice applies here. If you never want to progress or continue getting better at flying and understanding theory, do nothing. You will get better if you keep using the right tools and work on it. It might be slow, but it will happen!

Tenacity

Tenacity is the "never give up" attitude. We defined patience as forgiving yourself and giving yourself a chance; tenacity is a larger view, as it keeps the long-term goal in sight. This is the act of disciplining your mind to try again, to keep at it when everything isn't going well. The fact is that when you are learning to fly, your attention is divided between so many things that it can be overwhelming. There are so many different topics, procedures, and pieces of knowledge, and it is a delicate balance to maintain. This balance of learning and absorbing skills and info can be too much if you think about it negatively for too long.

The only way you will get better is to keep trying. The thing is, when you are going through this intense training, with so much pressure and so much information that has to be absorbed, you will feel like you are never getting better. You can fall into the pit of despair and give up.

But the truth is that you just can't see the progress when you are trying to hold all of that burden because it feels overwhelming. Part of tenacity is reflection, taking time to stop and look at where you started so you can see how far you have progressed. During the initial stage of training, it is vitally important for you to reflect on each flight and see how far you have come. This will build confidence and the foundation of your training. It's going to be hard at first, so do what you can to build your confidence and get a solid foundation. If you give up, you have a 100 percent chance of never reaching your goal; if you keep working on it, you have more than a 50 percent chance of achieving your goal. Never give up!

The final aspect of your personal emotional support is dealing with disappointment. When we don't perform the way we want to in a lesson, or when we have made a lot of mistakes, it is easy to give in to the feelings of despair and discouragement. And honestly, it's okay to feel that for a little bit; allow yourself to be angry and upset, but don't stay there. This dream of becoming a pilot is worth so much more than the momentary low you feel after a flight that didn't go well.

Reflecting

In my experience, when I had a flight during which I wasn't happy with my performance, I didn't need my instructor to tell me; I already knew I didn't do well. After that flight, I would leave the school and go and do something completely different from flying. It took my mind off the feelings of failure and allowed me the time and space to forgive the mistake. When I had distracted myself for enough time, I would go back in my mind to the flight. It doesn't matter where you do the reflection, it's just important to do it. You can just take time and go over the flight in your mind. Think about the procedure and what you did on your flight. Go back over it, think about your instructor's feedback, and see how you would do it differently. When we visualize the flight in reflection, we can slow it down and make the adjustments we can't make in real life. Remember, our planes don't have brakes in flight, so we adjust in our minds at a speed we can control by reflecting.

Visual reflection will help prepare you for the next flight. After you visualize, make some notes about what you did and how you will do it differently the next time. This does several things: it establishes the procedure in your mind, allows you as the student to see the differences, and reinforces the action in your mind before you have to do it again for real. Writing things down actually helps you put them in your mind and remember them. For me, it also keeps me focused enough to complete the task at hand. These practices help you take control of your own training. The instructor is there to guide you, keep you safe, and give you insight on flying, theory, and procedures. But realistically, you are the most familiar with yourself. You know how your brain works and what methods to use to make the information yours so it becomes a skill or second nature.

It is good practice to use these tactics after each flight, but it is especially important after a less-than-spectacular flight. This is a positive way to deal with negative results. Really, we always have a choice in how we deal with everything that happens in our lives. A note here about positivity: it is much easier to be negative than it is to be positive. This is a choice you have to make daily, and when things aren't going well, it is hard to be positive. These practices will help take a negative situation and put a positive spin on it. Sometimes life is just rotten, and bad things seem to all come at the same time, but with patience and tenacity, you can rise above it and excel.

If you are with a group of people, whether it's classmates, colleagues, or family, usually the negative one brings down everyone around them. Unfortunately, it doesn't work the other way around—the one positive one won't bring everyone up. It is your responsibility to take care of your mental environment to set yourself up for success. In the end, you are the one achieving your dream; no one else is doing it for you! As you start out on your new challenge, you will realize you are not starting at zero; you will bring a lot of transferrable skills with you from previous jobs, education, and just living and being. In fact, a lot of the experiences we have in our lives can be transferred to other areas we usually don't even think are related. These intangible skills will be discussed in the next chapter.

Chapter Summary:

- Succeeding takes time and self-forgiveness.
- Patience should first be practiced in our own training.
- Reflecting on lessons and events helps us improve, deal with disappointment, and move on.
- Never ever lose hold of your dream—never give up!

CHAPTER 9
E—EVALUATE:
COMING FULL CIRCLE

Evaluate is the best topic to end with because it puts the reader in the driver's seat, so to speak, and we have come full circle. Again, I would like to remind you that this framework is to give you control over yourself in a training environment. When the training system or instructor can't give you what you require, there are ways for you to find the information you need! The next few skills are included in the process of evaluating.

Multitasking

Multitasking is a skill we talk about a lot, but it can be misleading. Can a person actually do more than one thing at the same time? It really depends on what the tasks are, but typically, multitasking is more like "monitoring" multiple things at the same time. A very practical example is putting a load of laundry in the washer and then starting to chop vegetables for supper. An aviation-based example is flying an aircraft while looking for traffic or speaking on the radio at the same time.

Take a minute to think back to when you were a student in high school, working at your first job, or even driving your car. What are some instances when you were "doing," or monitoring, two things at the same time? When we drive, we are operating the car; listening to music, a podcast, or maybe a passenger; looking for traffic; and obeying all the rules of the road we have memorized. This is as close to flying as you can get while on the ground. This can also apply to riding a bike in traffic. Any time you have to operate something, navigate, remember the rules of the road, and stay alert to others, you are multitasking. We don't really think of it when we are used to it because it becomes second nature to us. This is the goal when becoming a pilot—memorizing rules and procedures until they become second nature so you can be alert and react to anything that is out of the ordinary on a flight.

In any training situation, regardless of the industry, the first two weeks to a month, you will learn the tasks that need to be done, the priorities of the job. Once you learn and become comfortable with these responsibilities, you will be able to multitask, or monitor several tasks at once. Expect to be slow at first, but you will progress and become faster and more efficient, especially if you have a plan to help yourself and use the ACE the RISK™ framework. How can we practice multitasking? Being aware of how we multitask is step one. Keep doing those tasks, but now, as you are aware of it, try to become more efficient while doing them. This will aid in mastering multitasking. This is a skill you will need, so practice now and carry it throughout every aspect of your life, especially as a pilot.

In one of my jobs, I had a chief pilot who really wanted me to succeed. He was more like a mentor than a boss. I was struggling a bit trying to get everything memorized in a very short time, and he suggested I practice while driving my car. He had learned how to juggle and would repeat his memory items while he was juggling! This was his method for learning two skills at the same time.

This simulates flying an aircraft and knowing what comes next for actions. Obviously, you can't physically touch controls in the aircraft when you are driving your car, but you can dictate to your brain what to do next. If you practice in the car, you can also slow down and take your time to really establish the memory items. This is vitally important for when you are in the aircraft and have to do the actions!

Task Prioritization

This brings us to the next point: How do we know what to do first, next, and further down the line? We learn to prioritize tasks. We learn this through trial and error in real life, and sometimes that can be a series of unfortunate events—but we don't usually forget it! In the aircraft, procedures and checklists help us know what to do in which order. Also, the phase of flight or nature of the problem will dictate where to start. For example, in a single-engine aircraft, when you have an engine fire, the first thing you want to do is cut off the fuel; that is the easiest and quickest action for the pilot to stop the fire. We don't have a lot of control over O_2 going to the engine, but we can control the fuel. A fire can't burn without fuel, so the fire will go out. This is a simple example, and the checklist for each particular aircraft is more detailed, but that is the initial action to do. When in on-the-job training, the trainer should tell you what order the tasks should be done in. If they don't, you can ask, and this is where observing them becomes important again. If you have watched them and think you know the order of importance, just confirm it with them. You can also make your own notes and lists to help you remember until you have mastered the skill.

My suggestion is that when you are learning the emergency procedures, for example, pull up the system it relates to and compare the two. If you know how the system works, the procedure will reflect why tasks are prioritized the way they are. Prioritizing is probably the skill we think about the least because it is done before we even think about it. When you are learning about it, pay attention to why the checklist is in the order it is. This will help establish in your memory the procedures and the normal, abnormal, and emergency checklists. It will also assist you in memorization because you will understand the *why* of the checklists.

Prioritizing the order of actions is not something we can compromise on. Follow the flight school or flying club's procedures. It's okay to ask questions, but follow the procedures. Prioritization is a skill companies will look for when you start job searching. The procedures are well thought out, and there are reasons they are done in a certain order. An example of this is when I would move an aircraft at a flight school I worked at. We had to have two people move the aircraft while bringing it in and out of the hangar. It took more time, but the reason this was a SOP (standard operating procedure) was because someone had moved an aircraft by themselves before and the wing hit the doorway and damaged the aircraft. Therefore, a new SOP was born. Each company should be respected for their specific rules and SOPs because there is a good reason for each one, although we may not know each specific reason..

Recall

Another intangible skill we use and don't think about is remembering and recalling techniques. In the movie *Akeelah and the Bee*, the technique the little girl initially uses to remember how to spell words is tapping her leg. Each of us has a way we retain knowledge, like our pattern of remembering. It will help you a lot if you find yours and then use it to "drill" the information into your brain. Regardless of your method of remembering, repetition is necessary to find your flow of information and how you imprint it on your brain.

Personally, when I study systems, I use the P-Logic™ system: purpose, parts, process, and problems (covered in chapter six). I like to make a simple drawing that connects the main parts, which helps me remember the parts and the process the system has to go through to function optimally. That way, when I study the problems or emergency checklist/SOP, I can quickly recall where the problem would be and what my actions should be to reduce risk and correctly deal with the problem. This method of finding your unique recall technique links back to chapter three, where we talked about personality and learning style tests. With this knowledge, specific to you, you will find the most efficient way to learn, remember, and recall! This is another step in taking charge of your learning! I am a visual learner, so my technique is to take notes, organize the notes in a way that makes a logical flow for my understanding, as well as add drawings and schematics if appropriate, and color code overlaps in knowledge. If you learn your method, you will set yourself way further ahead than you would normally be! Next, we are going to develop our internal skill set from personal awareness to intellectual awareness. We know our unique needs, so we'll look at required skills.

The next three skills I have labeled intellectual skills. We'll start with situational awareness. The skill of situational awareness is developed very young, actually. If you have driven a car, ridden a bike, or even played hide-and-seek, you have used your situational awareness skills. You become very aware of what is going on around you. Especially when playing hide-and-seek, you are extremely aware of where everyone is and where you are. That is really the best way to describe situational awareness. For aviation, we add where you want to be in a few minutes. Because our aircraft is always moving, we must include where we are now and where we will be soon.

Situational Awareness

Situational awareness is probably the most subtle skill you possess now, and you may not realize its importance. It will become very obvious when you start flying and have to watch for other aircraft in your airspace.

Here's a story to illustrate poor situational awareness. When I first moved to Beijing, my younger sister came to visit me. We had a wonderful time exploring the many interesting places in Beijing, meeting intriguing people, and enjoying the amazing food. One day, we were walking back from a restaurant that had the best burgers I ever had. The walk was about thirty minutes, and it was spitting a bit of rain off and on. This was an "on" part of the rain, so we had our umbrellas out. It was easier for each of us to have our own umbrella, so I had a larger one and she had a smaller one. The campus I lived on was surrounded by a wrought iron fence set in a half-stone wall and stone pillars every six feet or so. As we were walking on the sidewalk along this fence, her umbrella kept bumping mine. It wasn't a huge deal, just a small annoyance . . . that wouldn't stop. I finally hit her umbrella with mine and told her she had to be situationally aware, and if I ever got her to move planes, they wouldn't have any wingtips left. I had just finished saying this to her when my large umbrella got stuck between a stone pillar and a streetlamp. Since I was slightly annoyed, I was walking with great purpose, so it was a huge shock when my umbrella came to an abrupt stop! I looked over at my sister, my eyes big saucers of surprise, wanting some sort of explanation, and all I got was her literally doubled over with laughter. I had to join in because I immediately had to eat my words about situational awareness! It is a skill that is used in everyday life.

Situational awareness is especially important in a training environment as you learn the ropes. For example, imagine you are in an aircraft, solo, flying downwind and getting set up for an approach to land. You are multitasking by operating the aircraft, talking on the radio, and managing your path over the ground. But it doesn't stop there, you have to know where other traffic is coming from and going to, the expectations of the other pilots, and the expected actions from the air traffic controller instructions. In our everyday lives, we develop a pattern for filtering all information that we come across based on how it will affect us and how we'll react and protect ourselves. As a pilot, you have to start thinking of how your actions are going to affect other people.

In flight, you are responsible for your aircraft, how you may become a problem for another aircraft, and how to avoid them if they become a problem for you. This is why we have standard procedures and patterns that each pilot follows, so conflicts can be avoided. This all works smoothly if the procedures are understood and followed to the letter. This is not always the case if a pilot misunderstands, isn't sure where someone else is in the sky, or acts as if they are the most important one flying in a certain airspace. Remember, you don't have brakes, so you have to make decisions about what will happen in a couple of seconds or minutes. This is why situational awareness is essential.

Starting to develop situational awareness in your studies is a jump start for when you are flying. The easiest way to get used to using situational awareness is to take a moment to try to think things through from beginning to end. Here are a couple of examples:

- Example 1: During your studies, instead of trying to just learn facts and separate pieces of instruction, take the pieces of information and put them together as you learn them. It is like you are building a picture that will give you context, which will give a complete understanding. This understanding will aid in the memorization of procedures. This is situational awareness in a softer, more intellectual method.
- Example 2: You are in your aircraft flying into an airport that is uncontrolled, meaning it doesn't have a controller to give instructions or clearances. Each pilot within this airspace is responsible for avoiding other aircraft while still getting their tasks done. You have to follow the circuit, or traffic pattern, by physically flying the correct path and making the right radio calls. This all goes well if you are the only one in the circuit. But what if we introduce other aircraft that intend to enter the circuit? Now who has priority? Who goes first? This requires each pilot to state where they are in relation to the circuit. They then have to visually see one another so they can avoid one another. Finally, they have to verbally communicate what the intentions of each pilot are. Usually, what happens is one aircraft will extend a downwind or fly an orbit, or 360° circle, to give time and spacing for the other aircraft. Each pilot must start to think about how their actions are going to impact everyone in their vicinity. This is the result of learning situational awareness, a skill that will be a staple in your pilot skills toolbox.

Decision-Making

The next important skill is decision-making. In ground school, you will learn about making decisions, a step-by-step process for making these decisions, and how they apply to flights and your training. I won't get into the details on that point, as it will be covered in depth in your flight training, but I do want to provide an overall view of decisions and how you as a pilot will need to make them.

The very first function of making a decision is to know where you are now. If you don't know where you are at the moment, how can you know where you want to be in one minute, one hour, or one year? This concept goes back to chapter three, in which we talked about making your decision to become a pilot. First you have to know why you are here and where you are going. But breaking that down into smaller decisions is also important; when you come across an obstacle, instead of getting frustrated and allowing it to stop you, use it as a checkpoint on your journey. During my training, I ran out of money at about the IFR stage, so I was approximately three-quarters of the way through my training, and I didn't really have enough money to continue without asking for help. I thought about it for about a week and decided to ask my family if they could assist me. For that week, while I was thinking about asking them—or getting the courage really—I thought to myself the following:

1. I have gotten three-quarters of the way through my training and passed everything.
2. I love flying.
3. I don't have much further to go in my training to finish.
4. Am I going to let money stop me?

I asked one family member, and they agreed to help me out, so I continued my training and finished with all my licenses and a diploma. That was a decision that was made with much consideration and logical thinking. I had a support system that was able to help me out and could give advice as well as financial aid.

As a pilot, you won't always have a week to make a decision. Many decisions will need to be made under pressure and in a very short amount of time. But it comes back to the same basic method for reaching a conclusion: take a moment to recognize the problem, asking yourself, *Where am I right now?* Then, logically think about solutions. In the cockpit, if you are dealing with an emergency, you don't have time to write down a pros and cons list and think about every combination of actions and the results they will have. But you have knowledge and some experience, and you will have studied the emergency procedures, so you have context for how to react in each scenario.

Let's look at an example: You are working toward your commercial license. You are flying cross-country in a single-engine, piston-powered aircraft to practice navigation skills while gaining time for your CPL. You do your scan of all the instruments and notice the oil pressure is at the low end of the green arc (normally it is in the middle of the green arc). You have a decision to make! You have learned about this system using the P-Logic™ method (pages 63-65), so you have the knowledge.

What situation are you in right now?
- Could be an instrument indication error.
- Could be a leak in the oil system.

How should you deal with this problem?
- Continue to monitor the instruments.
- Start looking for a field to land (precautionary landing).
- Do nothing.

What is the best course of action? This depends on the situation.
- If you are downwind of the circuit and going to land, continue.
- If you are forty-five minutes away from an airport, start looking for a place to land.
- *Never* ignore the problem.
- *Never* assume it is only an indication problem; if it isn't, then you will have to think and act even faster than if you had been better prepared.

This is a general example of how using the knowledge and theory you learned on the ground assists in making a decision while you are in flight.

Life versus Reality

A word of advice: just because we don't want something bad to happen doesn't mean it won't. This is when your knowledge of the systems of the aircraft and how they work comes in. The procedures give you guidance on the actions to perform, and the confidence of having these two pieces should give you the nerve to execute a safe landing. You have memorized, practiced, and prepared for this! Your blood pressure may rise because you are in an abnormal situation, but you do have the skills to deal with the problem. This is why we practice emergencies so much during training.

Whenever you have to make a decision, whether it's aviation-based, related to your personal life, or part of any job, it is vital to know what the options are and how to conduct yourself to get the best outcome. Don't get caught up in the emotion of the decision; you'll have lots of time to deal with emotions later. Deal with the situation at hand and rely on your knowledge, experience, and ability. You don't get far into flight training before you realize you can actually fly a plane! Once you know you can fly the plane, it's time to work on fine-tuning your full set of skills.

In your career, whichever avenue you decide to work in—whether it be commercial airlines, medevac, charters, any other avenues for aviation, or in any industry—you will be surrounded by ways to inform yourself on the details of your industry, company, and their expected SOPs and behavior, as well as colleagues who can help you learn through their experiences. Absorb it all and keep yourself on the leading edge of your skills and current industry information. As previously stated for pilots, don't let the plane fly you; you fly the plane. This can be applied to any industry or job. Don't let the job control you; take control of the job!

How do we judge if our decisions were right or wrong? And what do we do with a "wrong" decision? An incorrect or less-than-ideal decision will lead to another decision. Going back to our previous example, if we just ignored the problem of low oil pressure, that could lead to an engine failure. Then your decision would be to do a forced approach, and you wouldn't have much choice, as it is more reactive than proactive. Informing yourself and making good decisions early is the best practice. In the initial stages of training, the consequences of poor decision-making are shown by learning what happens when you pass or exceed the limits of the aircraft, the airspace, and yourself. These consequences will be learned in the first part of any on-the-job training. After that initial training, it becomes the trainee's choice to make decisions that have positive or negative results. The following section talks about the set standards that we have to meet, either as tests or as certain benchmarks, in our chosen industry.

Test-Taking

The easiest, but also the most difficult, way to know if you are gaining knowledge or developing skills is by testing. As a rule, most people dislike taking tests; they can know the information backward and forward, but they get "testing nerves," and therefore, they don't perform as well as they could. This does not mean the person is not intelligent or hasn't met the standard. However, passing a written exam and a flight test is vital for licensing as a pilot.

You can't change your personality, nor can you completely control your nerves, so there are a few techniques you can use to prepare yourself for testing. For the government written exams (PPL, CPL, and IFR all have one each, while ATPL has two), you can do the review in your specific style of learning. Of course, this method should be used for every exam, but the government exams are the most in-depth. For example, if you are a visual learner, try to draw pictures or review pictures or schematics of systems and such. If you are an auditory learner, you can record yourself reading notes or find lesson videos to listen to. A kinesthetic learner will do best with watching videos on how things work together or with someone doing the task. Whichever way you learn, it helps to psychically write down notes either on paper or handwriting software. This will help engrave the knowledge in your mind.

Preparation for a flight test is a little different. The knowledge is still very important, but now passing also involves hand-eye coordination and motor skills. This is harder to practice because you only have a certain number of flights to do it in, and if you need more time, it can become expensive. The best way to prepare for this part is to "chair fly" and do visualization exercises. Get comfortable and visualize each skill. The standards and testing criteria are laid out clearly on the Transport Canada website with the marking scale, the exercises to be covered, and the prerequisites. This is what the instructor will use to teach you, what the examiner will use to test you, and what you should use to better prepare yourself. It's a good practice to know the limitations for the flight test early on in your training. If the standard is set early in training, as you do your solo practice flights, you should try to do each maneuver to the standard of the flight test. Then it won't be such a huge mountain when you actually get to flight review before your flight test. Looking at other industries, test-taking may not be as prevalent as in aviation, but there will be other standards that have to be met, and the same principles apply: prepare, keep calm, and do your best. You are evaluated on tasks you do every day!

While testing puts our nerves on edge, which is completely natural, there is a task we use every day and on every flight that makes each student nervous, especially in the beginning. This skill is communication, which we will take a closer look at next.

Communication

Effective communication is the most widely used, and abused, skill in the world, in my opinion. We communicate in every interaction we have in our work lives, in our personal lives, and within ourselves. There are many barriers to effective communication, and many times these barriers result in frustration, misunderstandings, and feelings of ill will. What follows is a structured breakdown of communication and an anecdote demonstrating miscommunication between two people who usually communicate well.

The communication process is vitally important. The first part of the process is easy: sending messages. We love to send messages or give information, but we don't do so well with receiving the message. So, what is the communication process? It's pretty simple: *sender ▶ message ▶ receiver ▶ feedback and interference* (something blocking the sending or receiving of the message).

The <u>sender</u> is the side who has the thought/message/input to give. The <u>message</u> is the information. The <u>receiver</u> is the person who is on the receiving end of the message. This is all very straightforward and obvious. The two more complicated parts are feedback and interference.

<u>Feedback</u> should be given to ensure the message has been received. The feedback can be verbal, a nod, a smile, or any indication you have heard the message. Feedback, or acknowledgment of hearing the message, doesn't automatically mean agreement with the message, it just means it's been heard. Asking for further explanation, or repeating the message, brings us to our last point: interference.

<u>Interference</u> is what can complicate the communication process. There are many reasons for interference: someone can't hear the sender, there's a language barrier, the volume of the message is too low, the receiver doesn't want to hear or listen, etc. Another form of interference is understanding the message from one perspective even though the sender meant it a different way. This perspective is influenced by a person's culture, upbringing, experiences, life attitudes, and adaptability to new or different ideas. For example, I had been living in China for several years and was back in Canada for a visit. Living in a different culture, you become used to the patterns of speech, even if you don't speak the language well. So, I was home for a visit, and my sister was telling me a story.

She said, "I was watching the news today at work, and there was this lady who drove her van into the ocean. Her kids were in the van and abandoned the van." She then looked at me, expecting a shocked expression. What she saw was a very puzzled and confused expression. What I heard was, "Her kids were in the van and a band in the van." I was very puzzled because I was trying to figure out how the lady, her kids, the band's instruments, and the band members could all fit in the van. Because I was trying to solve this problem of logic, I didn't process the story. After my sister explained that the woman abandoned the van, leaving it in the water, I finally understood, and we had a very long and loud laugh about it.

But this is the point: there were a couple of sources of interference here. As I was used to a language that uses words that are pictorial and have short sounds, getting stuck on a perceived illogical part and trying to figure that out made it so that I did not try to look for other possible interpretations.

In aviation, interference is definitely something we need to be aware of. It can be very subtle and hard to identify, but you as an individual should do your own detective work to find the cause of the interference and make moves to reduce or eliminate it. If someone doesn't understand, don't take it personally, as it's just an example of interference in the communication process and it's not usually done in malice.

Receiving and Listening

As mentioned previously, hearing, listening, agreeing, and understanding don't all mean the same thing. Someone can hear without doing the other three. Listening is when someone is paying attention to the message with the intention of contributing and moving the conversation forward. In other words, they're involved in the conversation and want to respond with their thoughts on the topic. For example, if you want to strengthen the sender's point by adding a story or an anecdote or make an alternate point to what the sender is saying.

Understanding and agreeing do not always happen with listening. If you are listening and trying to understand but don't, you can ask questions to clarify. Understanding involves a depth of listening and grasping the message and then making the message part of your knowledge base.

Agreeing is just relaying your opinion on a matter. Just because you listen doesn't mean you will agree, but the conversation can still continue. Agreement can be communicated nonverbally as well as verbally.

Ensuring the Message is Received

In aviation, we don't have a visual on the sender—everything is spoken communication. We have to memorize the specific radio language and the actions associated with this language. That is our responsibility as a pilot, and there is a radio license training that is part of the initial stages of getting your pilot license. How can we make sure the message is received? Well, it depends on the importance of the message. If it's a friendly conversation and someone is making small talk, confirmation isn't as necessary. If it is the tower controller giving you clearance for landing or an instruction to avoid an incident, it is vitally important. If we are in an emergency situation, messages are kept short, the sender speaks clearly, and simple words should be used. In a flight situation, we have specific radio language, and if there is an emergency, we use a scripted MAYDAY or PAN-PAN call. Using MAYDAY or PAN-PAN depends on how much time is required. If there is a very short time to land, we use

MAYDAY. If there is a little more time to land, we use PAN-PAN.

In aviation, it is important for the receiver to understand and respond, indicating the message is understood. Each verbal command, clearance, and instruction has an action associated with it. In this industry, we can't treat communication the same way we may in real life. Don't just answer verbally if you don't understand the controller's message. Clarify the instruction or message and then do the appropriate action for that instruction.

The key point to remember when using the communication process is to know your role and fulfill it well while reducing or eliminating interference. As the sender, be clear, be to the point (but not rude), and wait for feedback. As the receiver, listen carefully, respond (give feedback), and do the action or ask for clarification.

Lastly, be clear, talk slowly enough for anyone to understand, and use standard phraseology for the radio. Clear up misunderstandings and don't assume the person you are talking or sending a message to is thinking the same way you are; this assumption is the biggest cause for misunderstandings.

We have learned and talked about a lot of separate topics, skills, and knowledge so far. In the next chapter, we will put them all in context and give situations where they work together, both good and bad, so you can see the results of choosing how you decide to learn.

Chapter Summary:

- Be aware of the need for multitasking and work on becoming more efficient.
- Use your knowledge and checklists for task prioritization.
- Develop your own tools for recalling information.
- Situational awareness is a skill you use during every flight, and the need for it is the first step to developing it.
- Understand that reality and expectations are not always the same.
- Decisions are made using your knowledge, experience, and skills. Until you have experience, you will rely heavily on theory and knowledge.
- Use your specific tools to prepare for tests.
- Communication, relying on speech and listening, is very important. Learn the radio language well, as well as all the actions associated with the words.

CHAPTER 10
COMPLETING THE CIRCLE

The Big Picture

Now, how can you apply all this knowledge and these suggestions? I'm going to give you a few examples of a proactive student and a reactive student. It is the students' fourth flight in their private pilot license syllabus, and it is at 9:00 a.m.

Proactive	*Reactive*
Shows up more than an hour early for the flight.	Shows up at 9:02 a.m.
Starts looking at the weather reports and doing flight prep.	Waits for the instructor before starting flight prep.
Has done all the required reading and has a couple of questions to ask the instructor during the preflight briefing.	While waiting for the instructor, the student reads the material, which should have been done the previous night.
The last flight didn't go smoothly, but this student broke down the flight the next day, went over each item carefully, and has a game plan for this flight.	This student didn't have a good flight last flight, so they went home, got drunk, and complained about their instructor.

During the walk-around, noticed a wet spot under the plane and asked maintenance to check it out.	On the walk-around, noticed a wet spot under the plane and told themselves it was there before, from another plane.
When questioned by the instructor on the theory for the lesson, could explain it simply to indicate a basic understanding.	When questioned by the instructor on the theory for the lesson, hesitated and stumbled over the words, indicating proper study wasn't put into preparation for the flight.
During the flight, the student struggles a bit with the landing procedure but listens to the instructor's guidance and adjusts their actions to improve.	During the flight, when struggling with the landing procedure, the student gets frustrated, doesn't listen to the instructor's guidance, and performs poorly.
Fast-forward to the private flight test: student has studied, reflected, and visualized to correct the mistakes made on previous flights; reviewed the standards; and practiced to those standards during their solo flights. They pass their flight test. Although not perfect, they are deemed a safe and competent pilot and now have their private pilot license.	Fast-forward to the flight test: student spent minimal time preparing, tried to remember what the instructor said during debriefs over the past six months but had no reference to this feedback, and decided to try their luck and do the test although they didn't feel completely confident. They don't pass and blame it on the instructor and poor teaching instead of taking responsibility for their poor preparation.

Perfection versus Reality

The biggest goal of this book is to prepare you as a person and student in the art/science of studying so you will have the appropriate skills to thrive in any industry you choose. The main point is you will need to know *you*—your strengths and limitations, the ways you remember and recall information, and how you want your learning experience to go. You only have the power and ability to change or adapt yourself, not your instructor or your environment. You are going to learn emotional, intellectual, and hands-on skills; try to be aware and learn from your mistakes. Perfection is what we aim for but failure to reach it is part of the learning process and must be forgiven. Be teachable and a critical thinker. These are the tools that will make your learning journey make sense. Be efficient and hopefully enjoyable to teach as well on your journey to becoming a competent professional.

Feeling Secure in Using Your Toolbox

Let's go way back to chapter three, in which we talked about knowing your motivation. Why are you becoming a pilot? Why are you starting this new adventure?

To give an analogy, the reason you want to be a pilot is the toolbox, and the definition of success is the lid and lock. They are the foundations of the bridge, what you will build on for success, and you will keep developing these tools throughout your career. You have to keep going! The tools you put in this toolbox will depend on you and are uniquely yours, so own them and be proud of your uniqueness. Other people may seem to get it faster and more easily, but be true to your method. Although the way you develop the tools is unique to you, the tools themselves are similar across the board.

The Path You Will Take:
- the dream
- the obstacles
- the training
- creating solutions

This is the basic path for anyone pursuing a dream, a career, or greatness. The following tools are how you will streamline reaching this goal efficiently and intelligently. The ACE the RISK™ wheel is there to guide you in excelling in your chosen industry and as a person.

A – Assess
C – Construct
E – Evaluate
R – Relationships
I – Industry
S – Situations
K – Keynotes

We applied the ACE the RISK™ wheel to the aviation industry, specifically as a student pilot starting out.

Topic	Basic Framework	Aviation Application	Aviation-Specific Topics
You	YOU	You as pilot in command (PIC)	
ACE	ASSESS CONSTRUCT EVALUATE	Same but for an aviation context	
R	RELATIONSHIPS	Human elements	Human factors

I	INDUSTRY	Environment Operations Aircraft	Meteorology (weather) Navigation, radio communication, ATC Aircraft systems, theory of flight
S	SITUATIONS	Day-to-day tasks Lessons	Flight preparation and closing duties Flight skills for each lesson
K	KEYNOTES	Emotional skills Organizational skills Multitasking Intellectual skills	Patience, tenacity, disappointment Lists, graphics, note-taking Prioritizing, memory/recall techniques Situational awareness, decision-making, basic communication

Once you start recognizing and developing your individual skills and tools, they will have to fit into the industry you operate in. Just as the aviation industry is a highly regulated industry, due to safety requirements for the public, each industry has rules, regulations, and standards that must be maintained. The aviation industry has written exams, flight tests, and situational testing to maintain the safety benchmarks set to keep the industry safe. The industry you choose has benchmarks to reach and goals set out by companies within it. To be honest, we have the choice to meet these standards or not, but striving to be the best will make it go so much smoother and make your quality of life better.

There are two points to remember regarding government testing. The structure of the government written exams is there to make sure you can reason out an answer using pilot knowledge and logic. The flight test is to ensure your flight skills meet the parameters that make you a safe pilot, worthy of your license.

On the point of testing, it is human nature to always want to pass. If we don't, we usually have to pay more money to do the test again, and we probably thought we were ready for the exam the first time. So how do we deal with not passing the test? The first step is to allow yourself to be upset and disappointed; these are completely natural feelings, and it's okay to feel that way—for a period of time. Once you have gotten over the disappointment and are ready to prepare to retry, be honest with yourself. Sometimes we like to blame the teaching, examiner, or anything else, but even assuming all those things are true, you still have to find a way to meet the standard. We must find the reason we are not passing. Is it nerves? Is it a lack of skill? Is it something that was learned incorrectly?

Once you isolate the problem, you can focus your efforts and energy on that point. It is typical to not perform as well when being tested as when you are doing a lesson. Your instructor wants you to meet the standard perfectly when they are preparing you for the test. This may seem tedious to you, but they know and understand that you won't perform as well in a test environment. We overtrain so you'll be at standard during the exam, allowing for the worst-case scenario when your nerves affect your performance. So, when reviewing for the retest, really focus on where you think you need help so you are efficient.

Whether we pass or fail, we have succeeded, because a failure now becomes a learning experience. There will be another chance to pass if you fail. This is not a regular occurrence, but it is best to be prepared mentally for the eventuality you have to retest.

When we reflect on failing a test, that brings up the point of obstacles. We all have things in our lives that slow us down. In my experience, when there was a family illness, it stopped me from moving toward my goal of starting pilot training. I was disappointed but also understood that sometimes life requires us to put our goals on hold and deal with other important things that become our top priority.

Opportunity

So again, look at this as an opportunity to reflect on the goal and establish the reasons and motivation to pursue it. It is also okay to take time to deal with other priorities that pop up. Slow down, reflect, and enjoy the lull, because when it is time to pursue the goal again, your schedule is going to be busy and full. The only time your dreams and goals won't be there is when you give up on them, and that won't happen, right?

The last point I would like to touch on in this chapter is the building of confidence. Confidence is not attained by waking up one morning and saying, "I'm confident!" Unfortunately, it is not just a decision to become confident that makes you confident. We have all met people who act so confident you would think they do no wrong or never feel like they could do anything wrong. This can be a way to cover the fact that this person is not confident. Typically, a confident person shows their confidence by doing their job well. It comes back to being honest with yourself. Confidence is built by practicing the skill hands-on, practicing in your mind by visualizing, and by repetition of both. Perfectly practicing the skills to the standard set by the government and companies in your industry will gradually build confidence. Seeing success by doing things well and meeting the standards gives you satisfaction that you have accomplished the goal. This is confidence!

It's okay to not do everything perfectly, especially as a student. This is the time to build up the areas that need attention. Even during our careers as pilots, we are and should always be learning. Some people can see things from a different angle and give us a new way to see a bigger picture. An open mind is a tool that will actually help you as a pilot when responding to emergencies and thinking outside the box.

This confidence you build action by action, step by step, takes some time but is worth it. Try to enjoy the journey and understand that with important things, there is no shortcut. It is a process that has to be accomplished, so make it your own and thrive in your process.

To You, I Hand the Torch

Finally, my dear reader, I want to thank you for coming on this journey of my experience as I've shared the lessons I've learned to this point. I trust you have learned how to use the ACE the RISK™ wheel and apply it right away to your life or whatever training you will start or are in now. You as the student can now become a teacher, to yourself first. The underlying strategy is to be honest with yourself and dig out the places you need to focus on to become better.

Self-awareness is key and paramount to success, not perfection. Use perfection as your overall goal, but the step-by-step goals should be realistic and practical. Perfection is not practical as a short-term goal, and it's tenuous once achieved. In other words, if you reach perfection once, don't relax, because you will still have to work hard to keep it! But take heart, you will get there the more you practice and hone your skills.

Another goal I hope you picked up while reading this book is to become an example to the people who look up to you and become a role model to others who are on their journeys as well. We are all affected by and affect the people around us, so let's make that count! Be the hero in your own story! You can take control of your training, and although you are the student and need to rely on instructors to get the information you need, you can still do two-thirds of the work by organizing your information, finding efficient ways to remember and recall the information, and implementing ways to test yourself on and practice the information so it becomes yours.

There are many resources about this that can be found on the internet. My website, languagenavigator.com, breaks down the ACE the RISK™ wheel and gives specific learning tips and tricks as well as basic knowledge, taught in the same practical and logical way this book is written. The website also has links to government websites for the aviation industry.

Here are my final words of advice and wisdom for each of you: ask yourself the hard questions. Knowledge is power, starting with knowledge of yourself. Awareness and self-education are the first steps in a strong learning path and will only make your learning easier and more efficient. Finally, please, please be patient with yourself while still pushing yourself to achieve your goals for a fulfilling and rewarding career.

Chapter Summary:

- Build your foundation with your *why* and definition of success.
- Use the ACE the RISK™ wheel to create a plan.
- Learn to forgive yourself and use failure as a stepping stone.
- Take the opportunity and don't give up.
- My friends, it's time to go find your wings and catch your dreams!

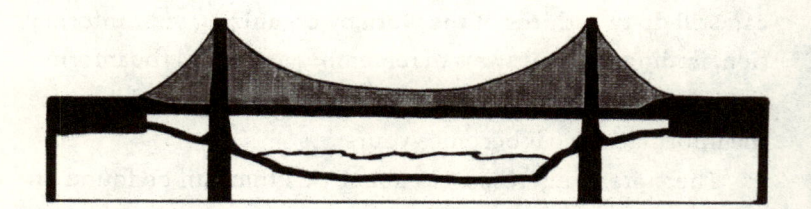

ACKNOWLEDGMENTS

First of all, I would like to thank my family for being consistently supportive even when I was working under the stress of deadlines. I would also like to thank the LA Writing team and Brands Through Books team—Ashley, Rikki, Chelsea, Jess, and Melody—for all their professional advice, guidance, and moral support.

Thank you also to the many people, past and present, who encouraged, mentored, and kept my perspective real—Ruty, Dad, Ramona, Patrick, Leanne, Bob, Laurie, Beth, Roz, Chad, Rachel, Jack Du, and Dean Tang. Without your wisdom, I wouldn't be where I am today.

And last but not least, thank you to my wonderful family, my faith, and God, who provided an environment to learn how to interact with people of all ages, personalities, and characters. *This* has been the fertile ground where I have learned to grow and become the person I am today. Thank you!

REBECCA BARKHOUSE is a Class 1 instructor and holds an airline transport pilot license (ATPL). She completed her Diploma in Aviation—Pilot course twenty years ago and has taught student pilots flight lessons in Canada since 2006. She spent nine years in China teaching aviation English and theory as well as general English. Rebecca is passionate about training and builds curriculums and learning materials to help a variety of students. She has flown medevac for six years and has been exposed to airline training.

Rebecca wanted to write this book to provide a guide for students or trainees as they start on a new adventure in school, university, or their career. The habits, tips, and methods she teaches she has learned herself through making mistakes and improving from them. She believes a person can't live long enough to make every mistake, so learn from hers!

Rebecca calls Nova Scotia, Canada, her home, but she does love to travel. She keeps a busy life, including hobbies like gardening, reading, doing jigsaw puzzles, and spending time with her friends and family!

To learn more about the author, please visit
https://languagenavigator.com.
To contact the author regarding speaking engagements, please email *rbarkhouse@languagenavigator.com.*
For all media inquiries or other questions, please email *rbarkhouse@languagenavigator.com.*

Printed in the USA
CPSIA information can be obtained
at www.ICGtesting.com
LVHW041639181024
794068LV00005B/79/J